Praise for **Isidore Century**
and
From the Coffee House of Jewish Dreamers:
Poems of the Weekly Torah Portions

"Isidore Century is a wonderful poet....
"His poems are brief stories: They're funny,
deeply observed, without pretension,
written with a knowingness and rhythm of
things old and new.
"Those related to Torah readings are poetic,
original midrashim, adding his distinctive
accent to the text."
– *The Jewish Week*

"Although I share Isidore's poetry with
the students in my weekly Bible class,
as an Orthodox rabbi, I would quickly be
tarred and feathered if I wrote a public
approbation."
– **name withheld by request**

"FROM THE COFFEE HOUSE OF JEWISH DREAMERS is so rich,
so full of life and has so much *ta'am*, tastiness,
that it is almost daunting to review."
– *Home Planet News*

From the **Coffee House** of **Jewish Dreamers**

Poems of the
weekly Torah portions

Isidore Century

Ben Yehuda Press
Teaneck, NJ

Published by Ben Yehuda Press
122 Ayers Court #1b
Teaneck, NJ 07666

http://www.BenYehudaPress.com

For permission to reprint, please contact:
Permissions, Ben Yehuda Press,
122 Ayers Court, 1B, Teaneck, NJ 07666.
permissions@BenYehudaPress.com.

Paperback edition:
ISBN13 978-0-9769862-8-7
ISBN   0-9769862-8-0

18 17 16   / 10 9 8 7 6 5 4 3

About the Poet

Born in 1926 as Irving Centor, Isidore Century is a practicing attorney living in New York City.

Century began writing poetry at the age of 45, following the encounter he describes in his "Journey to Coney Island" poems. His work has previously appeared in three chapbooks, in journals such as *Chelsea Review, Jewish Currents, and Midstream*; and in anthologies including *Borestone Mountain Poetry Awards 1976* and *Best Jewish Writing 2003*.

FROM THE COFFEE HOUSE OF JEWISH DREAMERS is the first book-length collection of Isidore Century's poetry. Poems spanning four decades are arranged in two back-to-back sections. POEMS OF WONDER AND WANDERING features the best of Century's previously-published material as well as some of his most recent poems, several published here for the first time. POEMS ON THE WEEKLY TORAH PORTION, among his newest work, offers double-takes on the familiar Biblical narrative.

Century's poems focus on aspects of the American Jewish experience neglected by many of his contemporaries in the world of New York letters. He writes of a lifetime suffering the scars inflicted by his immigrant parents, creating a raw poetry of the American Jewish experience—portraits of the Great Depression from a child's perspective.

Century's spiritual search leads him to seek his place in Israel and religious purchase among New York's Orthodox Jews. In such poems as "Stumbling to Jerusalem" and "Parallel Lines Never Meet," Century recounts his trips to Israel and wrestles with the promise of "returning" to the traditions he never experienced. It is a challenge that he never finally accepts nor outright rejects.

The poems in this volume were written in many of New York City's fine coffee shops, and the poet would like to acknowledge the waitresses for their kindness and patience.

Contents

Leviticus

Numbers

Deuteronomy

Note: The title of each poem is the title of the weekly Torah portion from which the poem was conceived. It may or may not have any relevance to the poem.

GENESIS

2

Bereshith

Cain (1)

It was my first case;
Murder!
I pleaded him innocent on the grounds of
  ignorance.
How could he know what a blow would do?
What did he or anyone know about death?
No one had died before.
I lost the case.
While Adam and Eve, the original sinners, were
  fighting over what punishment would fit the
  crime,
Cain ran away from home.
As a marked man,
he became a fugitive and a wanderer all his days.
He is still wandering,
I am still appealing.

Isidore Century

Cain (2)

He would have loved New York.
As a fugitive and wanderer
he could go to the movies,
eat Chinese and Italian food,
stroll in Central Park
and visit the Metropolitan Museum of Art.
Everyone would be too busy
to notice the mark;
  if they did,
would not want to get involved.
All he had to do
was mind his own business
and, oh yes,
control his temper.

Noach

I watched him hammering and sawing.
Why a ship? I asked. And so large;
we were miles from any ocean.
The story he told me, who would believe it?
But I believed his hammering and sawing
and hung around.
When he began to load the Ark,
clouds, like giant hippopotami,
began fighting for space in the sky.
I asked him to let me ship on.
Only family and animals,
that righteous nepotist answered.
I sneaked on board on the back of an elephant.
For forty days and more, I lived on animal food,
while he and his family had the best of
  everything.
I couldn't wait to get even.
As soon as the waters subsided, I seduced
a daughter-in-law and took her to Canaan,
where we begat a tribe of idol worshippers.

Isidore Century

Lech Lecha

Abraham (1)

I worked with Abraham in his father's idol-
  making business.
Whatever he knew about stone carving, I taught
  him,
  but his heart wasn't in his work.
He would stomp and shout all day,
"False idols. False idols."
I didn't think they were kosher either,
  but it was a living.
And for a boss's son, you couldn't find better.
He made me take coffee breaks,
  no work on Saturdays, a holiday always.

One morning, after his daily talk with his God,
he asked me to help him smash the idols.
I did not for one second think to ask him why.
I smashed.
As I did I had a revelation:
Abraham was a *mensch* one hundred percent,
because of this God he was always talking to.
When he left Haran I followed him
  into the land of Canaan.

Vayyera

Abraham (2)

As Abraham's number-one camel driver,
I was not two feet away when he pleaded with God
to save Sodom and Gomorrah.
First fifty, then forty, thirty, twenty, ten...
I told him go to five and stand pat.
But God was through with bargaining.
"Take it or leave it," He told Abraham.
And then Abraham couldn't find ten pious men!
What happened next you know already.
I ran one way, Lot another.
His wife, so worried for her daughters, looked
   back; she right away turned into a pillar of salt.
For why? She was, after all, a mother.
But who knows the ways of God.
Not even Abraham,
or he would have also spoken up for that poor
   woman.
If she had lived, Lot and her daughters would not
have done what they did.
It's in the Book if you're interested;
I'm ashamed to say it.
But what do I know about the ways of God?
I'm only a camel driver.

Isidore Century

Chayye Sarah

It was such a secret,
you will not find not one *midrash* from it.
She couldn't cook!
An *Eshet Hayil*, one hundred times;
she ran the household; she raised Isaac;
she did business with the caravans and Bedouins;
she was the sole breadwinner for the family;
she was some She!

But she couldn't fry an egg to save her life.
I did the cooking and I never told not one person.
For that *mitzvah* maybe,
an angel gave to me a recipe to make noodle *kugel*
with dates and raisins and pistachio nuts.

From the river Egypt to the Great River Euphrates
they heard from my *kugel* and everyone came to
Abraham's tent to buy.
It was like a restaurant, but no charge;
it is a gift from God, Abraham told them.
Those that asked who is God remained to be Israelites.
Abraham liked to say
we were a tribe of questioners,
but if not for my *kugel*,
we would not become a nation.

Toledoth

Rebecca

She was a nice Jewish girl,
but suffered from depression.
At night she had dreams of rotten red apples
from the Tree of the Knowledge of Good and Evil
falling on her head.
She had migraines,
she hated red.
When I emerged from the womb, she saw
her worst nightmare come true;
I, Esau, her first-born son, was as red as blood,
  as hairy as an orangutan.
As an old saying goes,
"If they that look at thee
doth a monster see,
a monster thee will be."
From the start she saw me to be a bad apple,
my twin brother, Jacob, was the apple of her eye.
Together they stole my father's blessing from me,
then covered up their theft
by making me a *midrash* monster.
Holy I am not,
nor am I the monster they made me out to be.
What did they expect of me,
a *yeshiva bucher*?

Isidore Century

Vayyetze

Jacob (1)

It was a condition of Jacob's service
that on pay day he play gin rummy with Laban,
a cardsharp, who took Jacob to the cleaners every time.
After fourteen years all Jacob had to show for his service
were two wives, two concubines and eleven children,
and not a dime to his name.

But God remembered Jacob
and sent an angel to help him be a winner.
After six more years
Jacob became a wealthy man.

Some years later,
when Jacob sojourned in Egypt,
Pharaoh, who loved to play gin rummy,
heard that Jacob had beaten Laban,
the premier gin rummy player of Haran.
He sent for Jacob.
Not wanting to deceive Pharoah
Jacob sent his gin rummy angel away.
He and Pharaoh played often,
hard-fought games,
each winning some and losing some;
no one kept score.

And Pharaoh offered him favors
which Jacob refused,
but he did ask for one:
that they not play on Saturday.

Vayyishlach

Dinah

She hung around Village coffee houses
with painters and sculptors, who were always high
on color, form, and space.
Of course it happened,
trouble.
She slept with a sculptor and brought dishonor
to Jacob and her family.
But there would be no swordpoint wedding!
The sculptor knew a good Israelite woman
when he had one; he asked Jacob for her hand.
Jacob consented on condition
that the males of the Village be circumcised.
It was done; however,
on the third night following the cutting,
when the pain was the greatest,
and the men at their weakest,
Simeon and Levi, behind Jacob's back,
slaughtered all the males and plundered the Village.
She went to Egypt with her brothers,
gave birth to a daughter, and disappeared
from Jewish history.

(Centuries later, she was resurrected
by Eddie Cantor, a Jewish star of the Broadway stage,
who found her in the State of Carolina,
where there was no one finer
than Dinah
Lee.)

Isidore Century

Vayyeshev

Joseph (1)

As soon as the sun set on *Shabbes*,
his brothers rode into town.
At the local Last Chance Saloon,
  they played seven-card poker with Egyptian camel
  drivers,
got drunk on wild cactus juice,
and spent the night at the two-bit cathouse.
From Joseph, Jacob heard all about their revels.
He unwisely gave Joseph a coat of too many colors
before sending him into the wilderness
to spy on his already jealous brothers
to whom he had told the dream
wherein they bowed down to him!
The coat was all they needed to see
to believe Joseph was tattling on them;
they sold him into slavery.

In Egypt, he interpreted dreams with such prescience,
he was appointed Viceroy by Pharaoh.
Twenty years and a famine later,
his brothers appeared before Joseph to buy food. And
as Joseph's dream foretold,
they bowed down to him.

Is there a *midrash* that says Jacob had a dream,
in which Joseph's journey and our sojourn in Egypt was
foreseen?

Torah Portions - Genesis

Mikketz

Joseph (2)

He knew that even in bad times
people liked to eat out.
He opened a cafeteria, the "Original Joe's":
the rich could have the choicest cuts of lamb or goat,
the poor, a low-cost falafel, and always
a bowl of chips, on the house.
In good or bad times, Joe's was *gemutlich*.
The manager, Ratner, made such a success.
"Original Joe's" was franchised all over the Middle East.
But when a new Pharaoh,
who was a *farbissener* anti-Israelite, was crowned,
he did not like *gemutlichkeit*,
he taxed the "Original Joe's" into bankruptcy.

Many centuries later, a descendant of Ratner,
opened a cafeteria on Second Avenue.
It wasn't fancy but fancy people ate there;
it was *gemutlich*.
If you only had the price for a bowl of cabbage soup,
a basket of warm rolls was placed at your table;
you could eat all the rolls you could eat,
no extra charge.
It was a tradition from the original "Original Joe's."

Isidore Century

Vayigash

Joseph (3)

I was Joseph's butler and valet,
his only confidant.
He was so busy feeding the whole world
he had no time for friends, or family.
"Your father lives not six days' journey away,"
I told him. "Let me go and inquire after him."
Such a stiff-neck he was, he would not change
his no to not even a maybe.
What did Jacob do, I wondered,
that Joseph should forsake him so?

A famine brought his brothers before him.
"Doth my father yet live?" he asked them.
When told he was,
what weeping and sobbing,
you could hear it all over the palace.
To celebrate, Joseph, who liked to cook,
created *gefilte fish,*
which to this day is served on Friday nights
with red or white horse radish, so strong,
it should make you cry like Joseph and his brothers.

Vayyechi

Jacob (2)

He never laughed;
like it was against the law.
What with a depressed mother,
a passive father, a brother
who was after him for stealing the blessing,
a father-in-law who switched wives on him,
his favorite son sold into slavery by his brothers,
and wrestling with an angel yet!
What was there to laugh about?
Every minute of his life was larger than life.
And there weren't any good Israelite jokes or comedians
making the rounds
of the fertile crescent vaudeville circuit
to give Jacob a good laugh.
But put this under your *yarmulke:*
Jacob never told anyone,
but secretly, he wished to be a gag writer,
who, in the world to come,
wrote jokes that made God laugh.

Isidore Century

EXODUS

Shemot

Moses (1)

He was a wanted man. The police
were after him for smiting an Egyptian
who was beating an Israelite.
Before, a Prince of Egypt,
now, a slave on the run.
He stole one of Pharaoh's horses
and rode for the hills into Midian territory,
where he could hide from everyone
but God, who was keeping an eye on him.

One day, as he rode around The Mountain,
he saw a burning bush;
it did not burn itself out.
From out of the fire came a voice:
"Moses, Moses, I am the God of your father,
the God of Abraham, Isaac, and Jacob.
You've heard of me, maybe?"
"From grandmother tales my nurse told me," Moses
    stammered.
"I have chosen you to lead the Israelites out of
    bondage."
"Why me?"
"I have a gut feeling about you."
"I don't think I want to get involved," Moses told God.
"It doesn't matter what you think.
It only matters what you choose."
"Do I have a choice?"

Isidore Century

"I gave everyone free will," God answered;
The bush was burning still;
God was waiting for an answer.
Who am I to say no to God, Moses thought.
"When do I begin?" he asked.
"You've begun. On your way; *zei gezunt.*"
"I don't speak Yiddish."
"O, I forgot. Go in good health."
Before Moses began the long walk back to Egypt,
he set his horse free.
It was the first step on the road to redemption.

Va-ayra

Moses (2)

"Let my people go," said Moses to Pharaoh,
"Not until I get my horse back."
"You have a thousand horses."
"It's the principle: Take a horse, you take a palace."
"I set it free in the mountains of Midian."
"Then find it and bring it back."
"Once free, forever free," Moses told him. "It's the
　principle."
"Power trumps principle every time," Pharaoh said.
"I have a higher power.
　The God of Abraham, Isaac and Jacob."
"Never heard of him."

But God had heard enough.
"Give him back his horse," He whispered to Moses,
　"or I'll have to do something I don't want to do."
"It's the principle." Moses said. shaking his head.
"Sometimes I regret giving man free will," God told
　Moses. "Principles can cause a lot of suffering."
"But what good is free will if we can't have principles?"
　asked Moses.
"What good are principles without power?" God replied.
"What good is a God without principles?" Moses asked.
"You need both," God said. "I'll show you."
He sent seven plagues down on the Egyptians:
Blood and Frogs and Gnats and Swarms of Wild Beasts,

Isidore Century

and Murrain and Boils and Hail.
Yet Pharaoh hardened his heart.
He would not let the Israelites go free.
"Three more plagues will do it," God told Moses.
 "The last one is a killer."
Moses wondered why
the Egyptian people
should suffer for Pharaoh's principles,
but he remained silent.

Bo

Moses (3)

The sight of blood made him sick,
and a whole river yet...
He became nauseous,
he developed ulcers.
Nine plagues later,
blood again,
of a sacrificial lamb,
on doorposts and lintels;
he saw red!
"Why should the Egyptian people suffer?"
  he cried out to God.
*"Why didn't the Egyptians cry out
  when the Israelites were suffering?"* God answered.
"Do you always answer a question with a question?"
*"Why shouldn't God answer a question with a
  question?"*
"Are there no answers?"
"Is there a beginning without an ending?"
Moses did not have a question with which to answer,
  but he had a revelation.
"There is a purpose to suffering?" he cried.
"Redemption."
and he had no more questions.

Isidore Century

Beshallach

Moses (4)

He couldn't swim.
He was afraid of water.
So were 600,000 former slaves.
And there was the Red Sea!
And there were Pharaoh's chariots!
"Go in," God said. " The water's fine."
He went in,
up to his ankles,
up to his knees,
up to his nose...
He took a faithful step;
the waters parted !
The people followed him onto dry land.
Behind them, "horse and rider He hurled into the sea."
On the way to the Promised Land.
in the pool at each oasis,
a few non-*yeshiva buchers* taught themselves to swim,
just in case they came to another Red Sea.
"You have to hope for miracles," they said,
    "but cannot rely on them."

(and it came to pass
many generations later,
one of their grandchildren, Marc Spitz,
became an Olympic swimming champion of champions.)

Yithro

Moses (5)

It was in all the newspapers:
the plagues, the parting of the Red Sea, the whole
    megillah...
When Moses returned to the land of Midian,
his father-in-law, Jethro, the High Priest,
had heard all about the miracles,
and came to greet and honor him.
But Moses bowed down to him.
"So, how's by you?" he asked.
"*It could be better. It could be worse*," Jethro
    answered. "*And you Moshe?*"
"It will get worse before it gets better," Moses
    replied.
"But right now we could all use a cup of coffee,"
    Moses said,
before introducing Jethro to Miriam and Aaron.
There is a *midrash* on a *midrash* that says:
over Turkish coffee and halvah
they taught Jethro to make *matzah*.
When a flock of quail nearby laid a batch of eggs,
Jethro had a revelation;
he fried pieces of *matzah* and eggs together:
they all feasted
on the first ever *matzah brei*.

Isidore Century

Mishpatim

Moses (6)

"It's the Big Ten or nothing," God told the Israelites.
Did we have a choice?
I'm not saying we didn't want it,
I'm not saying we wouldn't take it,
but when God makes you an offer can you refuse?
We didn't bargain.
We took. No questions asked.
But before we knew it,
we had Six Hundred and Thirteen *mitzvahs*.
And our priests, reading between the lines,
made a mountain of *mitzvahs*
out of every legal molehill.
Take for instance the *mitzvah*
not to seethe a lamb in it's mother's milk.
From that verse we couldn't mix milk and meat,
wo had to have separate sets of dishes,
to wash our hands before eating,
and to say a special blessing over every kind of food.
There was no end to what they could think of.
On top of all the *mitzvahs*, the priests
told us that every Israelite held the fate
of the Israelite nation in his or her hands.
If even one of us didn't do the right *mitzvah*
at the right time in the right way
the Israelite nation will be destroyed
in an instant!

We walked around on holy egg shells.
Not a minute could pass without saying a blessing,
or a prayer or doing a *mitzvah.*
Day and night we argued how and when to do it
  right.
Who wanted to be responsible
for destroying the Israelite nation?
If you saw and heard us you would think
we are a nation of *meshuggeners,*
and maybe we are, and were meant to be.

Isidore Century

Terumah

Moses (7)

"There are no free lunches," Moses said,
Nor miracles either, I told myself.
We owed God
for the Ten Plagues on the Egyptians
and rescuing us at the Red Sea.
But what did God want from us?
Only to do the *mitzvahs,*
and later to build a Tabernacle to his exact
  specifications:
No changes. No substitutions.
If that's all what He wants, I thought
 He won't get any arguments from me.
And Moses told us,
"If you make every stitch and stave and bracket
  with holy intent, you will receive a special bonus."
He wasn't talking about silver and gold;
he was talking about a reward in the world-to-
  come,
a once in a lifetime opportunity!
Redemption.
I grabbed it.
But no matter how many times Moses explained
  it,
the Tenth Plague made me feel
I had the blood of Egyptians on my hands.
So I offered up all my spoils,

and I worked on the Tabernacle like a dog,
day and night I worked,
until my hands became as bloody as the sacrificial
  lamb.
When the Tabernacle was finally standing
and the cloud came down to rest upon it,
I felt I had atoned for my sins in this world.
Whatever reward I receive in the world to come
will be gravy.

Isidore Century

Tetzaveh

Aaron

They say vestments make the man;
Whoever they are won't get any arguments from me.
Without the Holy Vestments
I cannot conduct a sacred service,
I cannot enter the Holy of Holies,
I am not the High Priest.
I am not who I am.

Though Moses did not need any holy vestments
to lead 600,000 Jews out of Egypt,
(for forty years he wore the same tunic
which Joshua cleaned and pressed like new every night),
yet if even Moses donned the Holy Vestments
it would not make him the High Priest;
he could not lead a sacred service,
nor enter the Holy of Holies on *Yom Kippur.*
That's my job.
Those are the rules!
I didn't make them,
I can' t change them.
The priests say God will never change them.
Can God create a stone he cannot lift?

Ki Thissa

Moses (8)

I knew we were in trouble
the minute I saw him
slipping and sliding down the mountain
like a man bringing two life and after-death tablets from God.
When he saw us dancing and singing
around a Golden Calf, was he mad!
I tried to explain:
"When you didn't come down from the mountain on time
we thought you were dead.
We needed someone or something to pray to.
Any idol in a storm," I said to lighten things up a little.
He didn't lighten up.
"*It's no j-j-joking matter.*" Moses stuttered.
"*There is no excuse for idol worship.*
It's a slap in G-G-God's face.
Besides I was on Israelite time;
Being late is already a minhag."

He smashed the two tablets to the ground.
He crushed the Golden Calf into a powder
which he mixed with enough water to fill 600,000 glasses.
He commanded us to drink.
We drank
I had heartburn for forty days and nights.
When he came back down the mountain
with two new tablets, I was cured of heartburn,
but not of guilt.
Always I'm a little gassy.

Isidore Century

Vayyakhel

Moses (9)

"You don't know the 11th Commandment?"
  Shlomo asked.
"*What is that?*" Motte answered.
"Thou shalt ask questions," Shlomo said.
"A *midrash* says it was written on the first set of tablets,
  but Moses was so angry with us,
  he forgot to write it on the second set."
"*Why did God give us this* mitzvah?"
"Because of free choice." Shlomo answered,
"He wanted we should be free to have the *chutzpah*
  to ask anyone anything we want."
"*You won't make a lot of friends that way,*" Motte said.
"You are 100% right, Motte,
  but if you don't ask, you don't learn."

So Motte asked Moses why his brother, Aaron,
was not punished for making the Golden Calf.
"*It was, after all, his idea, Moshe,*" Motte said.
Moses closed his eyes and prayed.
"What did you learn from this, Motte?" Shlomo asked.
"*Sometimes silence is the only answer.*"

Pekudey

Moses (10)

The *Shekhinah* is not a cleaning lady,
she doesn't do windows.
She has Her job, I have mine.
Her's is to be a holy presence in the Tabernacle.
Mine is cleaning and sweeping and mopping.
We are equals, but She is more equal.
The High Priest, Aaron, appointed me.
"*Why me?*" I asked him.
"You are the only woman who lays *tefillin*," he said.
"Moses wants to encourage the practice
so he has given you this honor."
Could I say no to Moses and Aaron?
Also I needed the money.

It may be an honor. but it's hard work.
As the Tabernacle travels through the wilderness,
it collects piles of sand and dirt.
I was about to tell Aaron he could take his honor and...
give it to a man,
when a scraggly brown and white dog,
no bigger than a fox, strayed into the Tabernacle.

Isidore Century

I gave him some water and scraps from the sacrifices;
he stayed.
What a cheerful companion,
as playful as a monkey.
But the priests, who do not like pets, objected:
they said the *Shekhinah* didn't like the dog.
I said if the *Shekhinah* didn't like it,
She would have said so.
They ordered me to take him to the wilderness of *Azazel*.
Over my dead body!

I took the case to the highest court,
to Moses himself.
"It's the dog and me, or get another cleaning lady," I
    argued.
"If women can lay *tefillin*," Moses decreed,
    "they can have dogs also."
I became a hero to the women,
yet only a few lay *tefillin*,
and fewer have dogs.
It's still a man's world.

LEVITICUS

Isidore Century

Vayyikra

I am not eating meat,
not chicken also,
not from the day my father took me to the Tabernacle
to teach me burnt offerings.
He cut the throat of a bullock:
its steaming blood came gushing
out of a lengthy, smiling gash;
the High Priest caught the blood in a vessel,
dipped his hands into it,
then dashed blood upon the altar and walls.
I began to feel sick.
When he cut the bullock into pieces and parts
and threw its organs and fat into a fire,
the smoke and stench filled the Tabernacle
like the smell of burning flesh and honey.
I threw up in the courtyard.
I became a vegetarian except, if on the table
there is pickled herring or chopped liver,
I give myself permission.
After all, I didn't take a vow.

Tzav

So every night, my husband, the High Priest,
comes home from a hard day's sacrifices.
He sometimes brings for dinner
a half-burnt steak or lamb chops;
it's allowed, but still,
I feel like I'm *shnorring* from God.
No matter, it's better than falafel again.

It does not pay much, the High Priest's job,
but it is steady, and I get *yichus* from it.
In the *souk*, when I go to buy
my eggs and cheese, my fruits and vegetables,
they take me right away.
I get bargain prices,
and for free, they give me eggplant,
which they know my husband loves,
when I cook it with cheese from the Galilee.

We manage comfortably,
even though the Holy Vestments,
with all the gold and precious stones,
which God ordered my husband to wear,
had to be made to order;
it cost an arm and a leg,
which came from our own pocket;
we will be paying out the tailor and jeweler
until God only knows when.

Isidore Century

I have no complaints, except
I have to wash the blood-stained, flesh-flecked,
smelly Holy Vestments
he comes home in every day.
The cleaning lady does not do Holy Vestments.

Shemini

To ask or not to ask,
that is out of the question.
My father asked, his father asked,
all our fathers asked,
it is tradition.
The priests say when two or more men are together,
it is a sin not to talk Torah; also,
we are so busy asking and answering and arguing,
it keeps us out of trouble;
we don't have a minute to play cards or chess,
or tell a few jokes, drink a little wine,
or to make a living.
But too much is too much;
we can become as crazy as the *yeshiva bucher*
who ran through the streets of the village shouting,
"Someone ask me a question.
   I have a wonderful answer."
And every question has a hundred answers,
at least.
A question I like to ask is,
   "Why did God take the lives of Aaron's sons?"
"*They were drunk in the Tabernacle,*" one answers.
"They disobeyed God's command," says another.

Isidore Century

"They offered up 'strange fire,'"
  a *chachem* puts his two shekels in.
My answer is,
that on the Inauguration Day of the Tabernacle
God came down to inspect the Holy of Holies.
By accident Aaron's sons walked in and saw His Face!
Not even Moses was allowed that.
When I first heard what happened to Aaron's sons
it shook my faith in God.
I became so frightened I ran to the Tabernacle
where I prayed and *shuckled* so hard
I was like a man having an epileptic fit.
I sprained my back.
My doctor prescribed complete bed rest.
"Don't dwell so much about Aaron's sons," he advised.
  "It happened because they were arrogant."
Another answer.
But he had no medicine to stop me from asking,
why bad things happen to good people.

Tazria/Metzora

My mother wanted always I should be a doctor,
but doctor's school would not take me.
So she got for me a scholarship to the *yeshiva*;
I became a priest.
I do *bar mitzvah*s, weddings, funerals,
I supervise circumcisions.
I'll never become rich but I'm happy in my work.
My mother says if I'm happy she's happy,
but she is always bragging to anyone
who listens anymore,
that to be a priest has more *yichus*
than to be a doctor, and besides, she says,
like the doctor who takes care of only the feet,
I am a doctor of the skin.

"My son the Doctor," she always begins.
Still, only I can decide
who has a rash or leprosy,
who shall be isolated for seven days,
and if and when they are cleansed.
Not even a dozen doctors together can make such a decision.
I have the last word,
except for my mother,
who has the last word
about everything.

Isidore Century

Acharey Mos

"Why me?" I asked the High Priest.
"*Why* not *you?*" he answered.
I didn't have a question to answer him,
so I became the official goat man who brings the
  scapegoat
into the wilderness of Azazel on *Yom Kippur.*
Once there, the shrieks and howls of sins
from *Yom Kippurs* past that were not redeemed,
could make you run for your life.
To me it's old business,
but to the goat, it's Satan laughing.
He digs his hoofs into the ground
and begins to bray like a mule, but he doesn't fool me.
By him, he may be a mule, but by me he's still a goat.
He refuses to move an inch.
As stubborn as he is I am more;
I'm not an Israelite for nothing.
I take the whip to the poor frightened creature
and drag him to the edge of a cliff
where I release him to Azazel.

When I return to the Tabernacle
I smell of sin and goat.
After the closing prayer and the blowing of the *shofar,*
all my sins are forgiven.
But the smell remains, and also a question:
why should an innocent goat,
also one of God's creatures,
suffer for our sins?

Torah Portions - Leviticus

Kedoshim

Three times a day I pray
to "guard my tongue from evil."
Yet every day, but *Shabbes*,
I betray my prayer,
I gossip;
I plead guilty with an explanation.

I am a peddler.
I go from village to village
selling trinkets and variety goods.
To my customers I am as welcome as a rich uncle.
Over a glass of tea or a *schnapps*
we bargain the price of needles,
a spool of thread, a pot or a pan.
Always they buy something.
But what they really want is gossip;
a juicy scandal makes them happy,
when they are happy they buy.
But Israelites don't much drink or gamble or whore,
so I have to stretch a rumor into a scandal.
Like the poor priest, whose name I don't mention,
who borrowed two shekels from the charity box,
to buy a loaf of bread for his family,
it became a story of how he gambled at dice
and became a wealthy landowner.

Isidore Century

Or about the cantor's wife,
who went to stay with her sick mother;
it became a story that she ran away with the butcher.

What can I do?
If I am not a gossip-monger
I would sell not even a button.
And how would I feed my children?
Thanks God for *Yom Kippur*.

Emor

It's hard to be an Israelite,
but to be a priest is, in two words, im-possible;
I wouldn't be a priest for a million shekels.
You live in a glass house,
the people watch you like a hawk.
As if Six Hundred and Thirteen *Mitzvahs* are not enough,
you have also to do sacrifices, weddings and funerals.
If you make a mistake, God forbid,
they throw stones at you.
For a *shlepper* like me, the *mitzvahs* are easy:
tefillin, fasting, *Shabbes* I can do on one foot.
And if I sin it's not a scandal,
like for the priest.
I sacrifice a bullock, a goat or a lamb
I repent,
I put money in the charity box,
I pray to God to forgive me.
If he doesn't, I have *Yom Kippur,*
for forgiveness insurance.
But *mitzvahs* from the heart,
they are on a higher rung than I can reach;
like bearing insults silently,
or loving thy neighbor as thyself
I don't even like my neighbor,
and he doesn't like me.
To love him is
Im-possible.

Isidore Century

Behar

What a salesman Moses!
And a stutterer yet.
He could have made a fortune selling used camels,
but he didn't want.
He wanted only to be in the God business,
to sell *mitzvahs* and real estate in the Promised Land.
So holy was this land, Moses told us,
every seventh year it had a Sabbath from planting and
  reaping.

He sold us a dream,
and though it foretold a formidable price,
we bought it.
He took no commission.

Bechukosai

If Shlomo is not in the middle of an argument,
he is not happy.
And by us there's no shortage of arguments or arguers.
One day he picketed the Tabernacle.
He carried sandwich boards that read,
"God is unfair to Israelites."
Before you could say *Aleph Bet*,
he was surrounded by a crowd of angry blackcoats.
"If you don't like Torah, go back to Egypt."
"Idol lover," "Self -hating Israelite," they shouted.
It was lucky for Shlomo that Aaron came by.
After stilling the crowd, he asked Shlomo,
"How is God unfair to Israelites?"
"The Torah says if an Israelite gathers wood on *Shabbes*,
if even only to keep his house and family warm,
he is to be stoned to death.
It's not like he is making a Golden Calf.
Who is he hurting?
And the punishment does not fit the sin."
"That law is only a warning to keep Shabbes,"
Aaron told Shlomo. *"No one ever was stoned for that
    transgression."*
"Warning, shmarning Aaron," Shlomo argued.
    "It's too frightening, and fear is not a good teacher."
"So how would you teach how holy Shabbes is?"
"By arguing," Shlomo answered.

Isidore Century

NUMBERS

Bamidbar

So who's counting
the men who are mustering for battle?
It is forbidden to count men
who are made in the image of God,
like they were heads of cattle.
So what to do?
Leave it to the Priests to find a way.
As each man came before Moses and Aaron
to receive the Priestly Blessing,
my team of scribes and I recorded their names and tribes,
from every man we collected one-half shekel,
given voluntarily as a preemptive atonement
for slaying an enemy on the battlefield.
Half shekels we can count.
Six hundred and three thousand and five-hundred fifty.
In one day!

Yet, all this mustering, collecting, and counting
caused me to pause, and wonder,
why
we had to prepare for war
to live in the Promised Land.

Isidore Century

Naso

Communiks we called them;
the long-haired young man and woman,
who came
from a commune by the Dead Sea to Jerusalem
to sell red and orange glazed pottery.
They wore white robes and white skullcaps,
they joined us for *mincha*,
but their ways were different than our ways;
they openly embraced,
they laughed and sang immodestly,
they were vegetarians.

One day there was a trial at the Tabernacle:
a woman, accused of adultery by her husband,
was ordered to drink a mixture of water and dirt
collected from the Tabernacle floor, and ink
bled into it from a parchment scroll
inscribed with curses.
If her belly swelled, stoning.
If not, she was sent home with her accuser.
The Communiks ran to the Tabernacle and protested,
"Trial by Ordeal is pagan." "Women are not slaves."
Out of nowhere scores of housewives appeared:
they banged pots and pans,
they threw tomatoes at the priests.
The trial was cancelled.

And though it is still the law,
Trial by Ordeal is no longer enforced.
But when the Communiks began speaking up
for mixed seating in the Tabernacle, the priests
threatened to ban them from Jerusalem:
open such a fence in the Torah, they warned,
and next the Communiks would have the *chutzpah*
to demand women priests.

Isidore Century

Behaalosecha

My *bobbe* did not like clear blue skies:
they had no faces,
they had no signs,
they had no dreams.
For her it was like having a glass of tea without sugar.
Better she liked a puff or pillow of white,
or a mountain of grey.
She would say they are descendants of the cloud
that led us through the wilderness,
and they are returning
to the Third Day of Creation
to become oceans, lakes and rivers again.
As she stroked my head, she said,
we are descendants of the first man and woman,
and we will return
to the Sixth Day of Creation,
to become another image of God.

Would my *bobbe* lie?

Shelach Lecha

All that keeps you from falling
is a thread of blue
that does not exist.
And yet,
you cling to it,
or it to you.
as Torah clings to Jews
who do not know an aleph from a bet.

Perhaps it is the command
to wear a thread of blue
you are clinging to,
or the mystery,
why God made the mollusks
from which the dye of blue was drawn
to become extinct
and allowed the command to remain.

I like to think
God is hiding them
in the deepest of deep aquifers.
When the Messiah arrives
and all the waters are redeemed,
the mollusks will reveal themselves
and from threads of blue,
I will weave
the first rung of Jacob's ladder.

Isidore Century

Korach

"Why am I all dressed in blue, Motte?" Shlomo said.
"You want to know? I'm doing *teshuvah*."
"So explain to me Shlomo, what teshuvah
  has to do with wearing blue?"
"I'll tell you one, two, three Motte," Shlomo answered.
"We were two hundred and fifty.
We all wore blue robes and blue skullcaps,
and stood with Korach against Moses.
'Are you more holy than we,' Korach challenged,
'that you can say we must wear a thread of blue
  although we are covered with blue from head to toe?' "
"And what did Moses say?" asked Motte.
"Not one word. He fell on his face and prayed.
Not a minute after, before my own eyes,
the earth split open and swallowed up
Korach and his followers."
"But not you, Shlomo. You had mazel."
"Maybe *mazel* and maybe not,
or maybe because I was not jealous of Moses or Aaron,
nor seeking a high position, like the rest.
I was only complaining, which God doesn't mind.
It shows I am thinking of Him.
But He had to give me a slap on the wrist,
so he made me a walking, talking thread of blue
to remind the Israelites that it wasn't *mazel*
that brought us out of bondage
in the land of Egypt."

Chukkas

There is no complaint department in the Tabernacle,
so I went directly to Moses.
"Why didn't God think of me," I asked him,
"when he sentenced my father and mother to die in the
    wilderness?
He must have known our silent boarder, Death,
would dispossess love right out of our tent.
And yet, God commands me
to love Him with all my heart and soul and might.
I wouldn't know love if it hit me in the face with a wet
    matzah."
For the first and only time I saw Moses smile.
"Neither I nor God can make you love Him," Moses said.
"But the next time I speak with Him,
I will ask Him to make a shiddach *with an* Eshet Hayil
    for you,
someone who will give you so much Israelite love
you will be getting hit with wet matzahs *in your face*
for the rest of your life."
"Is that a blessing or a curse?" I asked.
"That is not in my department," Moses replied.
He was not smiling.

Isidore Century

Balak

"You heard the story of Balaam and the ass?" asked Shlomo.
"Who hasn't?" Motte answered.
"So what do you think?"
"So what do you think?"
"God works in mysterious ways." Shlomo said.
"So what else is new?" said Motte.
"But you are such a Torah scholar, Shlomo,
explain to me why Balaam asks God
if he should go and curse the Jews,
and when God tells him to stay home
and mind his own business,
he has the chutzpah *to ask God to change his mind?"*
"To curse the Jews and be paid for it," Shlomo answered,
    "was an offer such an anti-Israelite could not refuse."
"So he went," Motte said.
"He went. But on the way
    his ass saw an angel and balked."
"Why an angel and an ass?" Motte asked.
"So Balaam would see that even an ass
    knows better than to go against God."
"Yet," Motte said, *"when Balaam saw the Tabernacle*
encircled by the flags and formations
of the Israelite encampment, he declaimed:
'How goodly are your tents, O Jacob.
Blessed are they that blesseth thee.
Curseth are they that curseth thee.'
So explain to me Shlomo, how one person
can bless us and be an anti-Israelite at the same time?"
"Like I said, God works in mysterious ways."

Torah Portions - Numbers

Pinchas

It was like placing a birthday cake
before a *Bar Mitzvah* boy,
who, because of a medical problem,
could not eat a sliver of it.
He could only imagine the taste
of chocolate, strawberries and whipped cream.
So it was with Moses.
He stood on top of Mt. Nebo;
Jericho, the River Jordan, the Judean Mountains,
the Promised Land lay before him,
but because of a spiritual problem
he could not put one foot on it,
net even for a second.
He could only imagine the taste of milk and
    honey,
he could only imagine redemption.

Isidore Century

Mattos/Massey

We went from here to there
and from there to here.
Two steps forward.
One step backward.
Sometimes one step forward,
two steps backward.
A journey of forty years,
no shortcuts.
We needed to be everywhere
to learn the lessons of here and there.
When we were near the Promised Land
Moses disappeared, but left a Book
to teach us how to be holy
in the Promised Land, and in the Diaspora,
how to live here and there.

DEUTERONOMY

Isidore Century

Devarim

What did I have to do with spies?
I was only a kid.
It was my father and mother.
They bet on a sure thing and lost to God.
He sentenced them and an entire generation of losers
to die in the wilderness,
perhaps, if you were lucky, before,
but not one minute more,
than forty years.

We marched, we camped, we prayed.
Day after day, a cloud,
night after night, a fire.
It was so boring some of us wanted to return to Egypt.
But Moses had a revelation:
you will not find it in any *midrash*:
he made up a game, two teams,
eleven men on a side,
who took turns trying to kick a large round ball
through the goal posts of the other team.
It was tribe against tribe.
If Moses wasn't the referee, bloodshed.
We were saved from boredom but not from each other.

When the last of the generation of the spies died,
we arrived at the Moab Mountains,
below, the River Jordan;

beyond, like a misty dream
waiting for us to dream it,
the Promised Land.
I wanted to run down the mountainside
and leap into the waters
but I couldn't swim.
I asked Moses to teach me;
he couldn't swim either,
He had a chance to learn when he was a Prince of
  Egypt,
but was afraid of the great Nile crocodile.
And now there was no time to learn,
he had to prepare a farewell speech.
It was always something with him:
Pharaoh, Sinai, the Golden Calf, the Spies;
he never found a minute to enjoy himself.
Maybe if he had a hobby,
like bird watching or pottery,
the Torah would have had some cheerful stories
or a few good Israelite jokes between the verses
 of Six Hundred and Thirteen *mitzvot*.

Isidore Century

Va-ethchanan

The priests have no crystal ball;
they're human like the rest of us.
Yet, though they weren't there,
they would like us to believe
only God was present
when Moses died on Mt. Nebo.
But among us stiff-necked Israelites priests
do not have the last word.
Besides,
Three witnesses have told us otherwise.
One, a blind man, heard Moses pray that God
allow him to enter the Promised Land,
not as one of rank but as a *shlepper*.
Another, a young shepherd,
said he saw Moses fall to his knees and ask God
to permit him to enter the Promised Land
due to his services to the Israelite people.
And Joshua, who was like a son to Moses,
said that Moses neither begged nor prayed,
but stood straight and tall,
hoping to the last minute
that God, as a matter of grace, would change His
 mind.
 Grace was not forthcoming.

Ekev

It was coming out of our ears.
For forty years, Death not withstanding,
all everyone talked about was the Promised Land;
we had the same dream in different colors.
A few of us didn't care if it was promised or not,
we only wanted to be out of the wilderness.
A rumor began that the Tree of the Knowledge of
  Good and Evil
had been transplanted to the Promised Land,
and, we would all have a second chance not
to bite the apple,
then mercifully be cleansed of the Big Sin.

When the last of the generation of the spies had died,
and Moses began his farewell speech,
a few of us, as naked as Adam and Eve,
stood on a mountain overlooking the River Jordan.
We were waiting for Moses to finish speaking
before streaking down the mountainside
and run across the Jordan valley,
into the Promised Land.
There we would find the Tree,
and as naked as Adam and Eve,
not bite the apple.

Isidore Century

But Moses kept talking;
he talked all day, he talked all night.
In the morning he was still talking;
we were freezing.
We decided the Tree would not run away,
it could wait for a warmer day.
We dressed, returned to our tents,
had coffee and warm buttered rolls.
And Moses was still talking.

Re'eh

Have you ever eaten vulture?
Or known anyone who has?
No you say.
Not me neither.
So why has God commanded us
not to eat what we don't eat?
You are saying it is his way
of telling us if we eat vulture
we will grow beaks and talons?
That's an old wives' tale.
You agree with me. Good.
So does it mean if I do not eat vulture,
I am doing a *mitzvah*?
And if I don't eat any of the forbidden foods
I am doing hundreds of *mitzvahs* every day?
You say they are very featherweight *mitzvahs*?
But they add up, yes?
And on the day of my final accounting,
as light as they may weigh,
they may tip the scales on my behalf.

It's better than a kick in the you know where.

Isidore Century

Shofetim

In Egypt, justice was a joke.
Like the one about the judge
who took an ounce of gold from defendant's lawyer,
then took two ounces of gold from plaintiff's lawyer.
The judge called defendant's lawyer into chambers
and informed him of the higher bribe.
"But, if you give me another ounce of gold,"
the judge said, "I'll give you a fair trial."

In the Promised Land,
Justice will be like bread.
Since Israelites cannot live by bread alone,
it will be buttered with mercy.

Ki Teitze

I was born as red as a bursting boil.
"Another Esau," my mother screamed.
"A curse," my father agreed.
They never forgave me.
I never forgave them.
By refusing to learn Aleph Bet,
by throwing my *tallis* and *tefillin* down the well,
by hunting for wild boar on *Shabbes*,
by stealing their money to buy wine and harlots,
I became the curse they wanted to see.
No *bar mitzvah* for me!
Instead, they took me to court where I was charged
with being a "wayward and rebellious" son.
If proven, death by stoning.
My father and mother testified to my dishonorable
  ways.
I did not testify.
What could I say? The charges were true.

But my Uncle Yitzhak came forward.
He told the court that from the day I was born
my father and mother labeled me
a wild animal, a donkey, leper, *momzer.*
They fed me only leftovers,
I slept in the shed with the animals.
I was beaten with a cat-o'-nine-tails.

Isidore Century

The court acquitted me on the grounds
the accusers did not have clean hands.
I was placed in my uncle's custody.
On the way to his house he bought
a chunk of chocolate vanilla pistachio halvah,
as big as a pie, and I, and his family,
had halvah sandwiches
on a new type of bread made from rye.

Ki Tavo

Why God promised us a land
made more unholy than Egypt
by the detestable sexual practices of the Canaanites
I did not know, so
I asked Moses.
"Because 600,000 Israelites heard His voice at Sinai,"
he answered,
"God entrusted us to make the unholy, holy."
"We're not so holy ourselves." I said,
  "Especially a backslider like me."
"Don't worry." Moses told me.
"By the sweat of your repentent brow
  you and the land will become holy."

But I worried.
In the wilderness when I sinned,
I would sacrifice a lamb or a goat;
and my sins were between me, the priest and God.
But in the Promised Land
I will every minute be looking over my shoulder
for the Holy Watchers, who love to catch
backsliders red-handed.
Even in the Promised Land
it will be hard to be an Israelite.

As the old saying goes:
I could live,
but they won't let me.

Isidore Century

Nitzavim

We had not yet set one foot on the Promised Land,
  already
 Moses is saying we will be leaving!
I thought it would be another Garden of Eden,
but this time, with a Book of do's and don'ts,
we would have learned our lesson,
and not bite the apple.
But Moses is saying many will bite
and those who bit and those who did not
will be booted out of the Promised Land,
head and *tefillin* first!
I asked Moses why we are going to a land
only to be kicked out of it.
"So we can return," he said.
"That's an answer?"
"It's the best I can do," Moses replied.
"But," he added, "when all Israelites everywhere
  observe one *Shabbes* together,
the Messiah will come
and lead us back to the Promised Land."
"Wouldn't it be better," I asked Moses,
*"to have a city of refuge for apple biters
instead of everyone going into exile?"*
He said it was a good idea
but God didn't mention it.

68

Vayelech

600,000 thirsty, quarrelsome Israelites,
clamoring for water.
What a commotion!
So God commanded Moses to do a *mitzvah*:
Speak to the rock and water will flow.
In his haste to quench their thirst
Moses smote the rock with his rod,
as he had done at Horeb.
For that mistake Moses was forbidden
to enter the Promised Land.
Why the rod then and not now?
The priests say it was a lesson for us all.
When God tells you what to do,
do it His way, or else,
it's the highway.
Not even Moses, especially Moses,
however good his intention,
can disobey a command from God.
But some of us learned another lesson;
no *mitzvah* shall go unpunished.

Isidore Century

Ha'azinu

He's singing! Yes, Moses.
After forty years in the wilderness.
It's like a revelation.
He would not win any prizes
but he can carry a tune,
and, thanks God, he doesn't stutter.
But why is he singing?
He's got good news and bad news.
The song is to soften the blow of the bad news,
which will hit us square on our unholy jaws.
In the Promised Land,
we will wax fat and follow no-gods,
we will bow to a frog princess,
and for these and other idolatries,
we will be kicked out of the land
with nothing but the *talleisim* on our backs.
And the good news:
as every sin contains the seed of a good deed,
so there is a refrain in his song
that contains a dream of our return
to the land of milk and honey.

Vezoth Ha-berachah

Not dead or alive
could Moses enter the Promised Land.

He stood on Mt. Nobo,
before him, the River Jordan, the Judean Mountains,
and beyond, a vision of Jerusalem.
He closed his eyes and died.
to be buried in an unmarked grave by God,
who does not need a *minyan* to say Kaddish.

When the Messiah comes,
the first thing he will do after a breakfast of lox and
  eggs
will be to have God lead him to Moses's grave,
and after Moses is resurrected,
with God's permission, the Messiah
will take Moses on a tour of the Promised Land.
After a day's touring,
over bowls of matzah ball soup,
made by God from His recipe Book,
Moses, the Messiah, and God,
Will write a *gevaldik* new Torah,
which will include the recipe for His holy soup.

Isidore Century

from the **Coffee House**
of **Jewish Dreamers**

Poems of
Wonder and Wandering

Isidore Century

Ben Yehuda Press
Teaneck, NJ

About the Poet

Born in 1926 as Irving Centor, Isidore Century is a practicing attorney living in New York City.

Century began writing poetry at the age of 45, following the encounter he describes in his "Journey to Coney Island" poems. His work has previously appeared in three chapbooks, in journals such as *Chelsea Review, Jewish Currents, and Midstream*; and in anthologies including *Borestone Mountain Poetry Awards 1976* and *Best Jewish Writing 2003*.

FROM THE COFFEE HOUSE OF JEWISH DREAMERS is the first book-length collection of Isidore Century's poetry. Poems spanning four decades are arranged in two back-to-back sections. POEMS OF WONDER AND WANDERING features the best of Century's previously-published material as well as some of his most recent poems, several published here for the first time. POEMS ON THE WEEKLY TORAH PORTION, among his newest work, offers double-takes on the familiar Biblical narrative.

Century's poems focus on aspects of the American Jewish experience neglected by many of his contemporaries in the world of New York letters. He writes of a lifetime suffering the scars inflicted by his immigrant parents, creating a raw poetry of the American Jewish experience—portraits of the Great Depression from a child's perspective.

Century's spiritual search leads him to seek his place in Israel and religious purchase among New York's Orthodox Jews. In such poems as "Stumbling to Jerusalem" and "Parallel Lines Never Meet," Century recounts his trips to Israel and wrestles with the promise of "returning" to the traditions he never experienced. It is a challenge that he never finally accepts nor outright rejects.

The poems in this volume were written in many of New York City's fine coffee shops, and the poet would like to acknowledge the waitresses for their kindness and patience.

Contents

The Visitor

Journey to Coney Island

Stories from the Thirties

Poems of Wonder and Wandering

Isidore Century

The Visitor

Poems of Wonder and Wandering

The Visitor

I did not know poetry.
Poetry knew me.
A distant cousin of Torah,
a survivor of psalm singers,
a long lost relative
from the Jewish Culture Club of Warsaw,
he knocked on the door one evening,
and all night long,
he and my father
sat in the kitchen
drinking *schnapps*,
telling tales of Rabbi Nachman,
and singing songs
from the deceased Yiddish Theatre
of Second Avenue.

Before I fell asleep,
he pinched me on the cheek
and sang me a *nigun*.
In the morning he was gone
and I wrote my first poem.

Isidore Century

Poem in Search of a Title

And finally, there is a dream
of a woman
into whose dream you enter,
and lying in the arms
of each other's dream,
together
you are redeemed.

Matzah

Like tulips and daffodils
they arrive each Spring,
boxes of them, on tables and shelves
and market places,
and though a non-believer
I cannot help but think that God
has had a hand in the making of them
out of nothing
but flour and water,
and sending us His furrowed holiday cards,
without signature or explanation,
from Egypt
by way of Jerusalem.

Isidore Century

Journey to Coney Island

Poems of Wonder and Wandering

Journey to Coney Island

In Coney Island
In April of my 45th year
I began to doubt my locations
I began to doubt
oceans.

the street signs, official,
formal in blue and white
were clear.
the roller coaster
curvy and indolent
sleeping in the springtime sun.
Brooklyn Jews wandering
like land locked sea gulls,
could testify to my presence
on Surf Avenue.

I am in Poland,
　　in the town where my father was born
　　in the sight of the parachute jump
　　in the synagogue praying
　　　with my fathers father
　　in a boardwalk pizza parlor
　　wearing a yellow arm band
　　carrying a black attache case,

It is clear to me now
I have been two journeys,
in all places, elsewhere,

Isidore Century

with all people, elsewhere,
like a dusty old Torah wandering
in search of a synagogue.

it is clear to me now
there were no accidents
only the crossings of an unknown journey.

In Poland
In April of my 45th year
while walking on the boardwalk
     with my father's father
I met a man wearing my life.

Journey to Coney Island (2)

In Coney Island
In April of my 45th year
I talked to a man
wearing my life.

"Who are you, and why
are you wearing my clothes"?

"I am Jacob Parefsky
once your downstairs neighbor
when you were a small boy
you came running each night to hear
a never ending made up story
of Berele and Schmerele
lost in the woods."

"Parefsky, Parefsky," I cried
hugging and kissing him
*Why did you move away and leave
me all alone with my mother and father?"*

"It was an adult thing.
Soon after, I died, and learned
I was your guardian angel.
I returned to Earth
and became your body.
It was my skin
that received the lashings
my bones that were broken

Isidore Century

running into cars.
It was my punishment, and my redemption.
Forgive me Yitzhak, forgive me
for deserting you."

"*Parefsky, Parefsky, I forgive you.*
Who else took me on his lap
told me stories
tossed candy kisses into my eager mouth.
I forgive you, but why, why
have you shown yourself now?"

"It is time you returned to your body
It is time your life ceases to be a dream."

We embraced in tears
He disappeared in my arms.

In Coney Island
In April of my 45th year
I began a new journey.

Journey to Coney Island (3)

Emerging from the dream
on the boardwalk at Coney Island,
like the first amphibian
crawling onto the shore
eyes blinking, unfamiliar
with unfiltered light
the sun
changing fathoms and ages of water
into warm bloodedness
into land appendages
possessed by new possessions
bones, blood, heartbeat, hair
my body, my own
like a first toy
the most important toy
I stand hypnotized by my hands
turning them over and over
my fingers moving
innocently
without motive
I am burdened by clothes.

Needing nakedness and a mirror
I run to the subway and home.

it is only now
standing naked in the mirror
I discover tiny scars
spotted

Isidore Century

like slivers of steel wool
along my arms and back.

it is only now
I remember the *konchuk**
a furious thing
raised high in my mother's sweated hand
whirring and striking.

it was not painful, then.

to see in my mothers' eyes
an executioner
is to feel no pain.

to see in her eyes
my murderer
is to be forever doubtful

to believe her eyes
is to believe in nothing again
not to believe her eyes
is to be always blind.

it is only now
returning to my body
her eyes have returned also.

----

* *konchuk* – cat o' nine tails, whip

Poems of Wonder and Wandering

Journey to Coney Island (4)

Searching the recorded madness
of her eyes upon my skin
for old records and films
seeking,
broken pieces of dead skin scrolls
fragments of milk
relics of embraces
before leaping off a wall
like Humpty Dumpty
into brokenness
to be pieced together
by the spit of dreams

Returning to her eyes
I return again to the wall
finding
yellowed messages of breast and lips
delivered and undelivered
hidden by survival
I see her eyes anew
her own leap from pain
into bearable madness.
we stand together now
before an eternal wailing wall
asking forgiveness.

Isidore Century

Journey to Coney Island (5)

On the golden sands at Coney Island
a man and boy
playing a game of catch, the ball
rising and falling gently
in perfect elliptical flight.

I see my father and I
in a vast and silent room
a rainbow colored ball,
neither caught nor thrown
flies between us.
we have no hands.

I return to playgrounds
stumbling after words
that fly like up and down staircases.
I learn to judge triangular flight.

My father
has clothed me in a coat of dreams
that smell, like he
of paint and sweat
tired muscle, cigarette.
He, whose sorrowed stance
was known to me
before I could stand or see,
has left a bag of toy defeats
that I have loved
like a fish in love with hooks.

Poems of Wonder and Wandering

in rooms of tomorrows he ran
to earnest meetings red with dreams.
child that I was
I forgave him all
the bastard Sundays, the untouched stumblings
but today, at Coney Island
the pain of elliptical flight
releasing the buried cries of broken winged days
is beyond forgiveness.

Isidore Century

On Rosh Hoshana

On Rosh Hoshana
in a synagogue in the wilderness
with merchant princes and indian traders,
I chanted prayers of the tribe of Israel
written in letters
    that jump, stoop and dance
    fight, trip and walk again.
    we were chosen
    we bend the knee

Stately spruce trees in green robes listened.
they judged not.

I came face to face with clouds
they asked not.

Leaping from a humpbacked word
my brother appeared.
he asked nothing but to take
his smaller hand
and walk with me a little way.
I cannot remember the beginnings of no.

of what infamy was he guilty
that I should burn our childhood bed —
mutilate his hand?

Freddy, Freddy,
If I could take you back
If I could take you back
to playgrounds and candystores
I would play basketball with you forever
there would be no end
to ice cream sodas
I would ask for your hand as well.

the pages turned themselves
behind the line "Thy mercy endureth forever"
he disappeared.

Shema Yisroel Adonoi Elihenu
in whom I have not believed,
thy clouds are full of cooling mercy
thy rain has fallen
upon me this day.

Isidore Century

Journey to Coney Island (6)

at an hour between sleeping and waking
I arrive at a terminal
by a wide river.
a place of beginnings and endings
Voyagers gather here
to move across unseen borders
from time clocks to dreams
from infinities to rectangles.

I have the power of invisibility.
old women clutch empty shopping bags
old men wash white socks
all stare at a separate piece of air
as tho' reading their biographies.

on the ferry, I take a post on the open deck
the sun
examines my face, its fingers
familiar and maternal, its light
breathing currents of red and warm
through my eyes, flowing
into arteries and veins
into the thin timepiece of networks and systems
of my journey.
I return a kiss.

An old black woman
asleep against a life buoy

pleads for her "Mama, Mama
Don't let them take me away,"
her fellow passengers study their own compasses.

a pigeon lands on the railing
one foot is missing.

On the other side of the deck
my childhood friends are shouting,
"Land Ho, Land Ho, Man the Yard Arms"
laughing, waving wooden swords
they leap over the side to catch a train.

In an aerial Tug of War
two sea gulls screech and fight
over a woman's breast.

a man, he is not my father
reads an Italian newspaper
the third finger of his left hand
has no top joint.
In Yiddish he tells me his is returning to Poland.

Fog
the passengers disappear
in the wheelhouse the captain, wearing dark glasses
wildly bangs a white cane against opaque windows
the ferry, a self-navigating sleep walker,
swiftly moves through dark waters
docking at Coney Island.

Isidore Century

I Embrace

I embrace the wild and mad dogs within me.
I embrace the yellow-eyed tiger
    raging through the underbrush of my smiles.
I embrace the befouler
    savagely trained into vanity
    and I embrace vanity also.
I embrace the outcast sibling
    howling in the distant hills beyond reason.
I embrace the shapeless monsters of the night
I have feared
I have hidden
I have been.
I embrace all manner of beast
    that I am.

Signs

a chassidic jew riding a motorcycle
it is a sign.

I dreamt my father was shaving me
it is a sign,

I.B. Singer reads Gimpel The Fool on the radio
it is a sign.

Old synagogues sing Pentacostal Hymns in
   Puerto Rican
A Black shoe shine man speaks to me in Yiddish
I find a copy of the Kabballah on the subway

there are signs everywhere this morning
I am sliding down silver banisters
from star to star on the Milky Way
each star has a stone marker
linking infinities of universes

I am connected,

there are signs

everywhere.

Isidore Century

Stories
from
the
Thirties

Poems of Wonder and Wandering

Jacob Parefsky

A downstairs neighbor,
each night would make up stories
of Berele and Shmerele lost in the woods.
The perils they faced!
Demons and bandits, witches and wolves.
How would they escape?
To be continued
in tomorrow's chapter.
But one day,
as Berele and Shmerele were being chased
by a giant ogre,
Mr. Parefsky moved away,
and Berele and Shmerele remain lost in the
   woods waiting for Mr. Parefsky to return
and save them.

Isidore Century

I Cash Clothes Man

He sang his one note song,
"I cash clothes,"
in the back yards of my childhood.
A ragged bundle of used clothes
strapped like a hunch to his back
compelled him to lean forward
and listen, ear to mouth,
to housewives haggling
over a nickel, the price
of a blouse or jacket.
A penny was a profit,
pity did not buy potatoes,
old was not like new.
He knew to the last snowflake
how many winters remained
in the life of an overcoat.
And yet, for a woman who
with trembling lips
could not speak on behalf of a dress
worn so desperately thin
its color had been drained of light,
he would give a few pennies.

My Aunt Rose said
he had an eye for damaged souls.

Big Lefty

In the small and sweaty world of the handball courts
I was his handicap,
the kid in the doubles game
who barely played at all
who dived onto stone
or crashed into the wall
to save a ball.
Big Lefty would say
"Good save, kid."
So I'd forget the beating at home
for tearing my pants again.
To hear Big Lefty say "Good save, kid,"
I'd go to hell itself to save a ball.

Isidore Century

Potatoes

I did not know Poland.
My father knew it and escaped.
It was never a subject of discussion.
His sister, Aunt Sadie told me
he refused to go to *cheder* or *shul*
despite being beaten by his father with a *konchuk*.
At sixteen he wore spats and a bowler
the only Jew in a gang
that smuggled chicory into Germany.
On *Yom Kippur* he could be seen dining
at the local saloon.
His father said Kaddish for him.
When the police broke up the gang
he hid in barns and forests
living on potatoes stolen nightly
from under the noses of farmers and dogs.

He came to America, an illegal,
and became a house painter.
After working all day, he would sit in his
  undershirt at the kitchen table
reading a Yiddish newspaper
and slowly, spoonful by quiet spoonful,
eat his blissful way through a bowl of boiled
  potatoes.
As silent as a coat of paint,
he kept his life to himself.
I did not know Poland.
I did not know my father.

Union Square

Once upon a May Day,
my father and I, and his comrades
from local 905 of the Painters Union
stood, with thousands more, to honor
Comrade Raven, a wounded hero of the Spanish
  Civil War,
and cheer "Red" Mike Quill, the president
of the subwaymen's union,
who brandishing his cane, and with a fiery
  brogue,
lambasted the bosses and top-hatted labor leaders.
Brass bands played, we sang
"The International," "Solidarity Forever," "Hold
  the Fort,"
and went home full of working-class hope.

Today there is a green market here, the Square
is crowded with shoppers and tent stalls.
There are no heroes or causes,
no banners or slogans,
and yet I hear the echoes of a crowd roaring,
"Free the Scottsboro Boys," "Free Tom Mooney;"
the songs resound in me still.

And in the sky, the pigeons, who cannot sing,
still bravely fly thirteen stories high,
where two men on a wooden, wind-ridden scaffold
are painting the window panes red.
Without wings they are at risk of flying;

Isidore Century

I recall my father and his comrades
playing rummy on our kitchen table
speaking solemnly of a fellow worker who fell,
and I wonder did I not know,
or did I not want to know,
that as I played basketball in Crotona Park,
my father was swinging high on a scaffold
to pay for the pair of Keds I wore.

Bar Mitzvah

My father took me fishing
with two left wing friends
from the Painters Union,
Sam and Morris Gaynor.
We rented a boat at City Island
and on a clear, chilly day
rowed out into Long Island Sound.
They gave me a turn at the oars.
When we arrived at a "good spot,"
we baited up and dropped our hand lines
to the bottom and began jigging.
I caught the first one,
a two pound blackfish
and received back-slapping *mazeltov*s.
I listened to talk and jokes
about strikes and scabs and scaffolds and Stalin
and caught a half dozen more.
When I had to go I stood up
and pissed over the side of the boat
as they did.
Lunch was cold salami sandwiches and hot red
  peppers.
My father poured Seagrams Seven into dixie cups
and handed out slices of Russian coffee cake.
I drank my first whiskey
and everyone wished me a Happy Birthday!

Isidore Century

Witness

I am a witness
to my Aunt Rose lighting Sabbath candles,
who was a witness to her mother
lighting Sabbath candles
who inherited this witnessing
from a long ago grandmother
who was a slave in Egypt,
who crossed the Red Sea,
who stood at Sinai,
who heard the telling of the commandments
and lit the first Sabbath candles.

I am a witness to my Aunt Rose
 lighting thousands of Sabbath candles
in the darkmost transmigrations of memory.

Short, short stories from the thirties

1.

A man came home from work.
"I'm dying," he told his wife.
  "*So die*," she said.
He lay down in bed and died.
Three months later
she committed suicide.

2.

Larry L. asked his mother for a nickel
to buy a comic book.
Because his mother didn't have a penny
in the whole house
she threw all his comic books
out of the fourth floor window
onto Bryant Avenue.

Isidore Century

3.

Mrs. Rosen went to court.
"Seven years ago," she told the judge,
"my husband went out to buy the *Daily News*
and never came back.
He loved me. If he was alive
he would have come back."
  "*Divorce granted.*"
Everyone knew her husband
was living with a widow
on Longfellow Avenue.

4.

From the 5th floor window
I dropped a slice of orange
down to Jerry Z.
in the courtyard below
who caught it in his mouth.
He ate half an orange
and never missed a slice.

A Fate Worse Than Death

In the East Bronx, during the Great Depression,
money was as scarce as tuxedos. When I cut
my head on an open kitchen cabinet door and
the blood began trickling down my forehead,
my mother saw green, not red. She grabbed
a broomstick and smashed a large hole in the
ceiling. Quickly she threw bits and chunks of
plaster on my head, then ran out into the hallway
and screamed for help.

Before the super and the neighbors came, she
pointed a finger right between my eyes and
warned me not to say one, not one, word, or I
would meet a fate worse than death.

One half-hour later, after the super and the
neighbors had witnessed the broken ceiling and
my bleeding, and after I had been bandaged
up, my mother gave me two cents to buy day-old
Hostess chocolate cupcakes.

We went to see Dr. Koulack the next day. Wise
in the ways of plaster-falling cases, he didn't ask
many questions. He looked at my head, patted
me on the cheek and gave me a lollipop. Then he
wrote something on a piece of stationery and gave
it to my mother. My mother said she would pay
him out of the settlement.

Three months later I was sitting in a courtroom.
A gigantic man in a black robe was examining
my head. He asked me if I had any headaches.
No, I said, as my mother had told me to or meet a

Isidore Century

fate worse than death. I began to cry. The judge apologized. "One hundred and fifty," he said to a man in a suit and a tie.

The man handed the judge some papers. He signed, my mother signed. As we left, the judge told my mother to vote the straight Democratic ticket.

That night, for the first time since my father had stopped working six months before, we had Chinese. My mother bought me two packages of Hostess cupcakes and gave me a dime to see *King Kong*.

King Kong was scary but I loved it. Except he reminded me of the gigantic judge and I worried if my mother and father did not vote the straight Democratic ticket I would meet a fate worse than death.

Bananas

My high school girl friend Milly Aronow used to
make me banana sandwiches. A chubby five foot
two, with eyes not of blue, but grey, like a cloud
that has its own reasons for going where its going.
She wore her shiny, dark hair in bangs. It gave
her a cute, innocent, look. But innocent she was
not. She had a saucy turn of lips and a teasing,
knowing air as though she knew all about sex but
wouldn't tell you all she knew. And she knew a
lot. At fifteen she could talk convincingly about
condoms, diaphragms, periods and deviate sexual
behavior. She even knew an abortionist, " just
in case." she would say. But there was never any
just in case with Milly. Necking was as far as she
went.

I used to take her to the movies Saturdays.
On Tuesdays and Fridays, when her mother
was doing an afternoon shift selling dishes at
Woolworths, we would neck, listen to music on
the radio and eat banana sandwiches. Sometimes,
onion or cucumber. She had shown me photos
which showed her wearing jodpurs and holding
the reins of a horse at her father's estate in New
Jersey. That made me think she was well off and
banana sandwiches were kind of neat.

Now, as I look back at those afternoons I see
things differently. I see how old the sofa bed she
slept in was, the cracked dishes, the rug that was
shabby and the blouses and dresses she wore

Isidore Century

had been washed and pressed so many times
they were as thin as paper. I used to think she
stole school supplies for the fun of it, not because
she hadn't the money to buy them. She was
poor, poorer than me. And I could kick myself for
not taking her to the Loew's Paradise as I had
promised.

  Promises, promises. If you don't keep them
they're like banana peels which you will step on
someday and fall flat on your remorse.

36

Fox Holes

Some mornings, while shaving, you appear in
the military cemetery at Coleville-su-mer, and
there, upon the still bunkered high bluffs above
Omaha Beach, you walk between white crosses
and stars of David, row by row. Below, the waves
crashing upon the silent sandy shore echo the
roar of gun and cannon, 6 June '44.

In November of that year you received your call
from the draft board.

Abe Passman and Herbie Cohen, who had
walked ashore with the 29th Division on D-Day,
cornered you in the back of the candy store.

"Dig deep, Sonny," they implored, "dig deep. If
a German tank overruns your fox hole, you'll be
safe."

They would know. At least Herbie would. Abe's
left hand, which he was flapping in your face,
was shattered on that, his first and only day in
combat. Herbie, two Purple Hearts later, was
awarded his third and last at St. Lo. With it a
ticket home, and a metal plate in his head for a
souvenir.

You were lucky. You missed the war by a month.

Some mornings you enter a cemetery in Queens,
and there, you walk between the monuments and
mausoleums of the burial societies of Pultusk
and Ostrolenko. Here, there is a grandmother
and grandfather, two pairs of aunts and uncles,

Isidore Century

assorted classes of cousins and landsmen of your
mother and father: Aunt Sadie always brought
you a giant Hershey bar, Uncle Harry, Turkish
halvah, Aunt Rose sneaked a pint of chocolate ice
cream into the hospital when your tonsils were
removed, Uncle Morris, the "rich uncle" always
slipped a quarter in your pocket when you weren't
looking.

   There was a price to pay for all this love. You
had to stand still for slobbering kisses and hugs
and knips on the cheek. Nor could you object
when they yiddishized and affectionized your
American nickname and called you Sonnele,
Sonnele.

   You wonder why you have to walk through
cemeteries to understand they were digging a
deep, deep fox hole in your heart to keep you safe
from German tanks.

Morning Service

While saying Kaddish for my father
he is standing beside me
praying and shaking so fervently
he is in another world.
When he was alive
he wouldn't be caught dead in a synagogue,
and here he is
all cleaned and pressed
in the navy blue suit he was buried in.

In the Painter's Union he was a minor official,
at home the same.
How he has changed;
a man performing a high-wire *mitzvah*
never seen before,
he is saying Kaddish for himself!
When I have concluded my prayers
I must ask him to explain.

I say Amen and look up.
He is no longer there.
On his vacated seat I find
an old hand-knit skullcap;
it smells of paint and sweat
and his brand of cigarette.

Isidore Century

My Father's Hands

even now,
knowing my skin
knowing my skin is raw
from his untouchings,
knowing his hands were frozen
by his father's untouchings,
knowing a gravestone
stands between us
like a wall between his room and mine

even now,
his calloused hands
reach towards me
from a graveyard of lost childhoods
asking
for my hands.

Flounder Fishing with Your Father on the Shrewsbury River

You rowed him out,
you rowed him in,
and never before or since
had you ever been
as father and son.
More like identical twins
born thirty years apart,
and playing a game
of hide and seek
in a rowboat
in the middle of a river.

Unraveling family hand lines,
you dropped them aimlessly into waters
too deep to catch the big ones
burrowing into the sandy silence
at the bottom of your lives.
You caught a few small keepers,
a pogrom, a *tsaddik*, a *shtetl*.
Not enough
to become flesh and blood.
But something is better than nothing.

You rowed him out,
you rowed him in.
In the twilight of his life,
he sat like a Yiddish casting of *The Thinker*
with a cigarette welded to his hand.

Isidore Century

Above his head, a pink
smoke ring hung in the air
like a gallows noose. He stared
at the water, wondering, you thought,
how a father and son, adrift
in the same boat for thirty years,
could have only caught
a few small keepers.

It was Ernest Hemingway, all his life
a fisherman, who said,
"You only have what you give away."
You have that day,
rowing with your father on the Shrewsbury River.
Not much of a keeper,
but something is better than nothing
to keep you on course
against the storms of silence
rising in the waters ahead.

Isidore Century

Portraits

Vincent Van Gogh

we are never the same
for his
madness.
for a single slash of wild yellow
yellows are never the same.
for the sanity of fire
for the sanity of sunflowers
for the sanity of insanity
we are changed
forever.

in the burning fields at Arles
mixing madness into oranges and reds
he challenged the sun.
he dared to create revelations.
no Icarus or Apollo he
flew beyond the blue boundaries of color
and fell,
a red-bearded eagle
screaming
at a white canvas.

he was to know
the antiseptic beds
of a stranger in his native land
and he became stranger still,
a nighttime visitor to cypress trees,
candles aflame in his sleepless hat.
he was to know,

Isidore Century

we must believe this,
that beyond the horizons of his canvas
was a world
where sanities and insanities
are simply colors
in fields of final yellow.

Hans Hoffman: Artist

in the beginning, a blue
rectangle of moon, at war
with earth orange skies, at odds
with the evens of your eyes.

You turned away
to the water lilies of Monet
(they were never to be the same)
only to return to the blue
rectangle . . . now a book.
You read a Chassidic tale:

    at a table an aged rabbi
    sits among his books
    listening to a pale-lipped disciple;
    "Rebbe, rebbe
    I was chosen in my poor *shtetl*
    to collect charities for the old,
    the infirm, the orphans.
    My collection box rattles with empty prayers
    my days are consumed dividing
    stale pieces of bread.
    At night, I dream of open mouths.
    My faith is breaking like the back
    of an old horse.
    Good rebbe, wise rebbe,
    what shall I do?"

Isidore Century

The rabbi stroked his beard
then pushing aside his books
he leaped upon the table
and danced.

Joseph Trumpeldor

even though a Jew,
the Czar decreed he receive
a sword and commission.
it never was easy for Jews
to achieve rank and position,
but the battle dispatches
could not be nobly ignored, and
he had lost an arm,
no small cost for one who planned
to resurrect a Jewish army
in Bar Kochba's land.

in America it was easier.
the gentiles not savage or throned,
allowing our fathers weapons — the laws of
  freedom —
resurrected ancient feral genes,
and we of the first generation
roamed the concrete canyons
of Brooklyn and the Bronx
like bands of horseless Apaches,
perennially clad in sneakers and armed
with basketball, football or baseball
we were joyous in all seaons.

Isidore Century

no wonder then our heroes
were Ruth and Gehrig and Dimaggio,
and when the great Hank Greenberg,
the Tiger of Detroit,
played at Yankee Stadium,
an army of Jewish men and boys
followed him, unaware of Trumpeldor's
last one-armed battle at Tel Hai,
unaware of the Ha-Shomer.

standing at his grave at Tel Hai
I wonder what Trumpeldor would have done
when the St. Louis sailed by our shores,
the smoke from her stacks
ominously rising in the sight of Yankee Stadium,
and where Trumpeldor would have led us
who needed his lost arm
even though we were Jews in America.

Tel Hai — a small museum and fort in the upper
Galilee.
Ha-Shomer — "the Watchmen," armed horsemen who
defended the early settlements in the upper Galilee,
St. Louis — an ocean liner, which in 1939, with 937
German Jewish refugees, was refused admittance to
the United States, and sailed back to Germany

Poems of Wonder and Wandering

Emmanuel Ringelblum, Diarist of the Warsaw Ghetto

In the footnotes of history,
it will be noted
he collected short, short stories
of life and death
and pinned them down
like spotted yellow butterflies,
into his diaries
to be read. . .
by whom, by whom?

There was so little room
for hope, and yet,
he buried his dead
in mass graves of milk cans,
believing, against the logic of fire,
that God would save a remnant,
who would return to dig
six million feet,
beneath the ashes and echoes
of vanished Jewish streets,
and resurrect a buried treasure
of golden butterflies.

Isidore Century

Souls

"So, why do you want to know
  if you will see your Aunt Rose
in the world to come?" the rabbi asked.
"My Aunt Rose, an Orthodox Jew,
loved her brother, my father;
she put up with me as a boarder
in my last year of Law School.
I came and went as I pleased,
I was so ungrateful
I refused to give her
the pleasure of sharing a Shabbes *dinner."*

The rabbi, taking a sip from his glass of tea,
looked thoughtfully at me.
"Not to not answer your question," he began,
"tell me how many people have lived and died
  since from Adam and Eve until today?"
"Millions?" I guess.
"Trillions," he said. "and they all had souls.
When God created heaven and earth,
He foresaw that trillions of souls would need a place to
  go
and He created the world to come,
so big, not even Einstein knows where it begins and
  ends,
But God, not wanting souls to be like refugees
drifting aimlessly around in space
created heavenly *shtetls*;
where a soul can go to be with *mishpocheh*.
So, for sure, there you will see your Aunt Rose."

Poems of Wonder and Wandering

Shabbes

I did not know *Shabbes.*
As a child I thought it was the name
of the bearded, black suited man,
who stood in front of the synagogue on Saturdays
cheerfully beckoning Jews:
"*Yidden.* Come in. Rest your souls."
As my father and I passed the synagogue by,
he tightened his grip on my hand and chuckled;
"I know *Shabbes* from Poland.
I like him but I can't live with him.
He doesn't let you rest a minute
from his holiness."
I wondered what mysterious delights
I might have found there,
yet, I lowered my eyes, and turned away,
ashamed that *Shabbes* looked so un-American.

Isidore Century

Stumbling to Jerusalem

Poems of Wonder and Wandering

Ben Gurion Airport

you arrive in a circle of guns.
reports of suicide squads appear
on pressurized retinas,
and the question why
you came arises answerless again.
but there is no time
for Jewish games.
there are necessities;
baggage, hotel and transport.
and surely, you cannot ask
at the information desk,
the sun carved Israeli face
cut from harder stone
than New York City Jewish rock,
and surely, you cannot ask
the crowd of faces, dark as camel drivers,
shouting taxi, taxi.
the bus to Jerusalem growls impatiently,
the cacophonous line conducts you
as quick as an eighth note
to a seat beside a
machine gun
in the lap of a sleeping soldier,
its muzzle gaping at your jumping intestines,
which oddly settle down.

the bus roars away and the soldier awakes.
he asks for a light.
a few words exchanged through the desert night,

Isidore Century

America, birthplace, occupation,
and there is no time
to ask him why.
he falls asleep, the muzzle of his gun
dumbly staring at your unasked question.

Yiddish

I was born in the land of Yiddish,
a place where nouns and verbs,
like its soups and breads,
were of mixed origins.
How I left, and when, I do not remember.
I seemed to have leapt from the mother country
into a land full of children speaking
Ringolivio, Skelly, and punch ball.
I became a citizen of English.

Years later I visited the holy land
and found *mishpocheh* from the *shtetl* of Pultusk.
I was smothered with embraces
as warm and comforting as *cholent*.
I could not speak Hebrew;
they could not speak English,
and as though I had never been away,
I returned to the land of Yiddish.

Isidore Century

Land Of Milk And Honey

When all the stones refuse to be thrown,
when all the guns refuse to shoot,
a great snow will fall across the land
for seven days and seven nights.
There will be silence and sleep
as in the beginning of silence and sleep,
the old dreams, wounded by war, will heal.
On the eighth day, to offend no one,
we will dig ourselves out of the old memories
and light bonfires in the valleys and hills;
there will be great potato roasts,
we will sing songs never heard before
and when we learn each other's words
for peace and forgiveness,
remove the potatoes from the fires and laugh
at one another as we burn our hands peeling
  them
and char our lips eating them.
The lakes and rivers will be full of fish,
the fields abounding in sunflowers.
We will build small houses on small parcels of
  land.
In our synagogues, churches and mosques
we will pray for snow every year.

The Wall

And where is the beginning of redemption.
O where, o where, but in Jerusalem.
A nonbelieving Jew
you stand at The Wall
like a golden calf seeking redemption,
and the Jewish punishment for such chutzpah,
a golden nail in your shoe.

Beside you at The Wall, a Jew
is davening. A blue tattoo
half hidden by *tefillin*
tells you all,
and nothing.
in spite of Auschwitz and Buchenwald,
or because of them,
he stands at The Wall
among *shnorrers* and rabbis
and you, an American Jew
to whom *tefillin* is as alien
as an Apache rain dance,
he turns to you. *Nu* . . .
A Jew meets a Jew, you talk
like old army buddies bound
by ancient campaigns in Egypt and Sinai.
He has paid his diaspora dues
six million fold, and you,
a penny's worth of prayer.
"HaShem takes pennies too," he tells you.
"And yet, to take a golden nail from a shoe,

Isidore Century

a penny can nothing do.
Only by leaping from The Wall
only by believing that *HaShem*
will save you from the fall.
Nu?"

Nu.
Oh how blue his blue tattoo,
and you an Apache Jew . . .
You pick up a *tallis* and *tefillin* from a stall,
you climb to the top of The Wall
and take a Jewish swan dive,
yarmulke, tallis, tefillin and all:
you land safely
into the prayers of *shnorrers* and rabbis.
Only the *shnorrers* pay attention to you;
leapers from The Wall are nothing new.
You take a place beside The Wall
and wrap *tefillin* 'round arms and head.
You say the *Shema*. The words,
like fledgling sparrows leaving the nest
take clumsy but accurate flight.
Still more Apache than Jew,
you hear an old refrain,
Siz shver tsu zein a yid,
It's hard to be a Jew.
(It's not easy to be an Apache either.)
You have to keep leaping from The Wall
to keep the golden nail out of your shoe.

Poems of Wonder and Wandering

Jerusalem Snapshots

There is no place to hide in Jerusalem.
Eternal questions are left at your doorsteps
like abandoned babies
crying for answers.
They are blessings in disguise.

At an outdoor cafe
beggars rattle their cups in your face
and by a peculiar Jewish alchemy
of repentance and good deeds,
you pay a high price
for a tin shield against punishment.

A madness for learning.
Yeshivahs everywhere.
Rabbis on biblical soap boxes
teach the 613 ways to redemption
through Torah, Mishnah, and Gemara.
You become lost
in a Judean wilderness
between Kabbalah and Tel Aviv.

On a bus to the Wall
a stranger rebukes you
for not wearing a *yarmulke.*
When you confess to eating lobster
he raises his eyes heavensward,
asks the price of your shoes
and invites you to *Shabbes* lunch.

Isidore Century

The sun pins your shadow to the Wall.
it begins to *shuckle*
like a feverish Chassid pleading
for the Messiah to come at once.
You did not know you were an Orthodox Jew.

You are playing hide and seek with God.
If God is God He will find you
and maybe He will explain
why you have to play a game
to find Him.

Jerusalem

El Aksa Mosque

shoes
standing in the doorway
like sinners
waiting to be resouled.

Damascus Gate

at the Wailing Wall
I don a *yarmulke.*
at the Mosque of Omar
I remove my shoes.
at the Church of the Holy Sepulchre
I light a candle.
at this fortressed gate
the moneychangers demand no rituals.
all passports are valid.

Via Dolorosa

the young but balding priest
leading our tour along
the Stations of the Cross
raised his tired voice
above shouts and screams
of children and shopkeepers,
to remind us that He
carried the Cross for us all.

Isidore Century

Visions

on the hills of Jerusalem, the streets
that long ago wandered in from the desert
have remained like sightless beggars,
waiting in the dust of the twentieth century
for visions
to appear in their brass cups.

if you wander here,
lay aside your travel guide,
lay aside your reasons,
remember Abraham
and study the light of Jerusalem skies.
remember Monet
and study the colors of light on Jerusalem stone.
remember the streets that have remained
and follow them into the desert
and turn again.
you will see Jerusalem
is a city of ancient visions
reminding us that without our Jerusalems
we are all wanderers in the dark.

Sightseeing, Jerusalem

There are no straight lines in Jerusalem.
Crows and buses travel over ancient routes
that circle the city like *tefillin*
around the arms of our grandfathers.
The streets, named after famous and not so
  famous Jews,
from Abraham to Hillel Zeitlin,
give you a shorthand tour of Jewish history.
As you try to understand it,
the bus you are riding on winds around
the ramparts of the Old City to Dung Gate.
"Last stop.
Everybody off.
Bathrooms across the plaza.
The Wall, to the right."

At the foot of the Wall, a bearded blackcoat
ignoring your New York Yankee baseball cap,
shouts *mincha* in your face and pulls you
into a *minyan* for the afternoon prayer.
Mincha said, *mincha* done,
kvitles submitted, *tzedaka* given,
you start to walk away from being Jewish
but are mugged by a memory
of your Yiddish speaking Aunt Sadie,
who, when you came home from the Army,
threw her fat, lumpy arms around your neck
and cried all over you, *"Ich dank Gott, Ich dank
  Gott."*

Isidore Century

Embarrassed by such Jewish potato love,
you politely pushed her aside to be with your
  friends.
Now, at this most Jewish of places,
you burst into tears and plant your sobbing lips
against a pyramid size stone and pray
your kiss will be transmitted to Aunt Sadie in the
  other world.

Returning to the bus stop under an anaesthetic of
  repentance,
you do not know where to go.
The #1 bus decides for you;
it takes you to the Street of Prophets.
A single street sign is the only official reminder
of their prophecies, that and the falafel man,
who has been at his stand so long
people say he is a descendant of Isaiah.
With a smile as big as an Iraqi pita bread,
he hands you a falafel ball to taste.
"Better you won't find in Jerusalem," he tells you.
You don't argue with a descendant of Isaiah.

You stand at a stand on the Street of Prophets
eating a falafel; it has a taste of prophecy.
And though you do not know which bus or route
  to take,
you are on the right path.

Poems of Wonder and Wandering

Mea Shearim

in the market place of Mea Shearim,
a handful of old men and women
are seated on wooden boxes,
brass cups asleep in pious hands.
there are no beggars in Mea Shearim
no passerby is asked
yet no one refuses the cup's command.

in a musty synagogue one afternoon
while Kaddish prayers were read
I watched a madman pass from mourner to
  mourner
as easily as pages turning
in the Book's required reading.
every mourner gave a coin.

my friend Moe Freed has told me
of a shopkeeper he knows in Tel Aviv,
who each morning sets out ten coins
on a shelf by the entrance door.
one by one, ten men appear
and take one coin.
they come with the store.

Isidore Century

Cafe Alaska

I did not know Treblinka.
in the Cafe Alaska
I met a man who knew it well.
why he chose my American ear to tell
of it I cannot say.
in truth I wanted not to hear.
in blood I could not turn away.

I listened to events
sworn to, stamped and verified
and yet, can any affidavits,
waxed and sealed and ribboned, recover
the bare bones of unbelievable truth?
perhaps a show of slides.
one face per second of the six million...

I did not know Treblinka.
in the Cafe Alaska
I met a man who is a witness,
and now I am a witness to his witness.
I have seen some pictures, some records, yes
I will testify, for if I do not
know Treblinka,
how can I say Kaddish for my father?

The Cafe Alaska was a popular cafe in Jerusalem

Poems of Wonder and Wandering

Jaffa

The early settlers who came by boat
would see the Crusader Citadel,
and then the flies.
They were not surprised,
Russia was full of citadels and flies.
After a hurried glass of tea
they ran off to the Galilee
to search for deeds
of their ancient ancestors.

Now, on the ramparts of the citadel,
beneath a peppermint candy canopy,
you are served a demi-tasse:
the sun appropriately sets
into a most historic sea,
and at the harbor's stony mouth
lies Andromedas' rock,
the very place of legend.
it is all so civilized,
so civilized, you are quite surprised
to find a footnote in the travel guide,
no legend this;
the Greeks, in the 2nd century B.C.,
sank a boatload of Jews in this very port.

Isidore Century

And there you are,
like an English nobleman discovering
a *yarmulke* on his peeraged head,
and hearing an alien voice within him sigh,
siz schver tsu zein a yid,
it's hard to be a Jew,
the well worn Yiddish words
surprisingly comfortable, as though
they were waiting for you
in the Port of Jaffa
beneath a peppermint candy canopy.

Standing on the Shore
of the Galilee

If Jesus could swim,
he may have been standing on this very spot
before diving in.
But if he could not,
it might explain why he walked on water
to go to wherever he was going.

I dive in.
Far out on the sea,
two heads bearing *yarmulkes*
bob up and down in uncharted waters:
And they are arguing!
"What should we do," one asks, "if God forbid,
there is another flood?"
"*We will build arks as large as cruise ships,*"
    the other answers.
"Not with my money," the questioner replies.
"Better with God's help we will develop gills
and learn to live underwater."

Drawn to such thinkers and dreamers,
I begin to swim towards them,
but not being trained in the tradition,
the currents are too strong.
I return to shore and look back;
the yarmulkes are out of sight,

I like to believe the swimmers are still swimming,
    that Jesus is still walking
towards the same distant shore.

Isidore Century

Sea of Galilee

and you would trade it all
trade it all
to lie beneath a tall palm tree
at an orange lilac sunset
watching the spangled blue
Smyrna Kingfisher skim
above its silver, shimmering twin
in the purpled waters below
its journey into night.

where gray bearded fishing boats
anchored deep, light
ancestral lamps of brass
whose red and amber glass
keep an ancient watch
over travelers in the night;
and before going to sleep,
you set out nets full of dreams.

Kvitles

We place a note,
no larger than a folded olive leaf,
into a crack in the Wall, a request to God to bless
  the departed or the sick.
Visitors, believers, non-believers
and in-betweeners as I, all place *kvitles* in the Wall.
And though every crack is as packed
as a shul on *Yom Kippur,*
God reads and removes a handful every day
so there will always be room for more.
There are rabbis who say
the mortar that binds the stones together are the
  kvitles.
If not for them, the Wall would fall,
and with it bring down the Temple Mount
and the Mosques of Omar and Al Aksa.
And the rabbis also say,
that as *kvitles* are to the Wall,
so are Torahs, strewn throughout the Diaspora, the
  mortar that binds heaven and earth.

Isidore Century

Friedman Beach — Tel Aviv

in the undeveloped light at sunrise,
a small but steady crowd
of men and women
mostly over sixty-five,
jog and swim, bend and stretch,
creak and groan, complain and gossip,
but mostly laugh,
as though being alive each morning
is the funniest joke they know.

Hooded Crows, Jerusalem

Their hoods,
as black as my grandfather's *yarmulke*,
cannot disguise who they are;

Penitent Jews,
they fly from tree to tree,
cawing and cackling,
pretending to look for food.

When they believe no one is looking,
they silently glide away to cemeteries
searching for the names of people they have harmed.

Finding one, they form a minyan on the gravestone
and make such a racket saying Kaddish
they wake up the dead
and ask for forgiveness

Isidore Century

Digging in Jerusalem

and when you return to America
and resume
the favored embraces of accustomed suits,
the reasoned comfort of seasoned shoes
waiting like leathery old passports
to reenter carpeted places,
you resume your resumptions,
as though bathing in the Dead Sea
(also waiting for redemption)
had not stocked your dreams with invisible fish
that nightly alter established sleeping positions,
stretching muscle, pulling bones and splitting
the inner seams of old embraces,
tightening your shoes in carpeted places.
and while resuming your resumptions
you are digging, digging, digging in Jerusalem
for a proper fit,
and only a tailor or shoemaker in Jerusalem
can make you a proper fit;
it is an endless dig.

Isidore Century

Wanderings

Poems of Wonder and Wandering

Beginnings

And where do you begin,
And where do you begin?
You go to the rabbis.
"With *Aleph Bet*," says one.
"*With* tefillin," says another.
"To them, don't listen," says a third in Yiddish.
"With *Shabbes* begin."
You are partial to the mother tongue;
on *Shabbes* you visit his shul.
In a sea of *talleisim*,
yarmulkes bob up and down like mooring buoys.
In the balcony, women in ornate hats
sit before twelve stained-glass windows,
taller than the Patriarchs of myth.
You are handed a *tallis*, a *yarmulke*,
and a prayer book in Hebrew and English.
And where do you begin?
A man beside you tells you the page;
but the *davening* is in Hebrew
and you quickly lose your place.
A hopeless case, you wander
to a shul on the Upper West Side;
it has services for beginners.
You learn the *Aleph Bet*,
the *Shema* and the *Amidah*, and yet,
as the rabbis all agree,
you cannot teach the blind to see,
nor can Torah, Mishnah, and Gemarah
teach you to believe in God.

Isidore Century

Wanderings

You wander from shul to shul
like a Jewish peddler
carrying a bag of curses and wounds,
inflicted with *konchuk** and tongue
by a close-to-crazy mother
who was beating and screaming
at the beasts and demons that pursued her.
And like rats running through the house of her
  madness,
the landlord at the door,
the debts at the grocery store,
your father, out of work again,
hiding behind the Daily Worker,
you were left with a bag of curses and wounds
which you could not sell, nor tell to God,
who wanted to buy your entire stock in trade
to redeem you.
No sale!
You do not trust his promissory note.
As a silent partner to your mother and father,
He stood aside as they sold you a bill of no goods
which you bought, which you bought
lock, stock, and a barrel of non-kosher pickles.
Caveat Emptor! Let the buyer beware.
Neither infancy nor ignorance is an excuse.

If they that look at me
doth a leper see,

_____

* cat o' nine tails

a leper I will be.
A secret vow,
so secret you did not see
the two-faced image you came to be;
you saw what you wanted to see,
a baby blue-eyed do-gooder,
a prize-winning nice guy,
all wrapped up in red ribbons,
who wouldn't hurt a fly,
not a fly. People though,
got in in their ever-loving necks.
Especially so those who came too close:
You hit them below the belt
with your bag of curses and wounds.
And to what aim, to what aim?
Spite, spite and spite again;
getting even for the leper you became
was worth the two-faced game.
What if you hadn't any nose?
What if you hadn't any face?
it was the only game you could play,
until you ran out of players.

And yet, and yet,
God, too, can play a game.
In spite of spite, in spite of shame,
or because of it,
He cast a glimmer of light into the pit.
O how can you explain the darkness
is the night waiting for a light.
Grasping it,

Isidore Century

you did not ask Him to explain.
You shouldered your bag of curses and wounds
and climbed out of the pit.

You wander from shul to shul
you wander from rabbi to rabbi.
Bearded and beardless,
holy and not so holy,
when you open your bag of curses and wounds
they brush it aside
as though to look inside
would turn them into pillars of salt.
And what of my sins you ask.
No excuses they say.
And my stinking character traits?
Did you lay *tefillin* today, they answer.
No saviors, they
dismiss your bag of curses and wounds
with a shrug of pious disdain.
And once again your old buddy spite,
like a laughing golem in the night,
lurches out of your bag again
and urges you to run, run
to the nearest church and convert.
All that is required of you
to he unburdened of your bag of curses and
  wounds
is to give up your *yarmulke*
to Jesus, himself a Jew.
You choose your *yarmulke*,
or it chooses you.

Poems of Wonder and Wandering

There is something about being a Jew .
You do not observe Shabbes,
you do not keep kosher,
and yet
you are counted in minyano,
you are needed to be a Jew.
Perhaps it is nothing more than that.
You cannot give up your Jewish hat,
nor give up your bag of curses and wounds
to anyone but God, in whom you hope
but do not believe,
and only He,
at a time and place of His choosing,
will redeem you.
Perhaps God, too,
needs you to be a Jew.

Isidore Century

You Take Your Golems with You

You take your golems with you;
a gang of unwanted siblings,
as tough as hunchbacks,
as fierce as fever
they besiege your nights
with howls of hope
and pleas for laughter.
Remorse,
never a friend of yours,
trampling over your life
like a runaway horse,
broke every hopeful bone in your body,
save one, a prayer to God
to redeem your golems from exile.
Now that they have been resurrected,
what would you do without them,
their grotesque blessings,
their almost unbearable forgiveness?
The shoe of redemption
is on the other foot
as if it matters
who is redeeming who.

Stopover 1

In shuls as large as cathedrals,
you lose sight of candles;
in shuls as small as *shtibls*,
you lose sight of stars,
and yet, and yet, and stubbornly yet,
you stumble from shul to shul.

Not with sticks and not with stones
do the Black Coats greet
your beardless face.
Eighteen eyebrows, raised
like a holy firing squad,
pin you down like a Jewish butterfly
to a bench in the rear of the shul,
and with a mournful sigh
they turn their pious eyes away
and begin to pray,
leaving you with your stillborn *Yiddishkayt*
fluttering blindly toward redemption.
You are wanted but not welcome.
If being the tenth man is a *mitzvah*
you will get your reward elsewhere.

Still, you are glad to be here.
Davening is *davening*.
Believer or not.
The buzzings and hummings
of the straight-edged Hebrew prayers
open your bag of curses and wounds,

Isidore Century

and your gang of forsaken golems
come howling and crying out
to forgive and bless you.
You embrace them all.
You bless them all.
Here, in the rear of the shul,
your golems have been redeemed,
and no holy firing squad can harm them.

Stopover 2

You stumble after the light.
Rabbis in striped blue and white
prayer shawls tell you
Torah is the light.
Yet even they disagree,
at times so vehemently
over the meaning of a verse,
they stone and curse
one another like Jacobs and Esaus
returned to fight over the birthright.
You wonder if Torah
is not a Coney Island
with 600,000 neon lights.

Family, friends old and new
laugh at your half-kosher *Yiddishkayt*.
They want a bearded old Jew
or a lobster-loving Yid.
And when they ask you for proof,
they want miracles.
O how can you explain
the 23rd Psalm
to proof-needers?
At one moment it is nothing
more than a poem and a prayer,
the next, a glimmer of light.
How can you explain stumbling
after a rainbow
in the darkest of night?

Isidore Century

The Return

You begin to browse in Jewish
bookstores on Essex Street. Orthodox
shopkeepers suspect your bareheaded Yiddish
conceals a Cossack wearing eyeglasses.
At each book stall
you stand on the shore of a sea of words;
the waters do not part. On Essex Street
the only miracles are in pickle barrels.
You purchase another mezuzah;
they lie on your desk like fallen stones.

Nightly, standing beside a wall,
you are accosted by an elderly Jew.
His fingers encircle your arm
like *tefillin* of steel.
"Let me say a *brucha* for you," he says.
"No, thank you, not at this moment."
"It wont cost."
"I don't feel like it at this moment."
"A Jew not to want a *brucha.*"
"Not now."
"If not now, when?"
An angel of death flies over us. You submit
a coin that thanklessly slides
into a bottomless pocket.
"I wont to let you go without a *brucha.*"
But stubbornness you have inherited as well as
  he,
and eye to Jewish eye

Poems of Wonder and Wandering

you engage in a tug of wills
until a one-eyed stranger hands you his card:
"Jews! Arm Yourselves!
Vladimir Jabotinsky."

One day, on Avenue A,
you are waiting for a bus.
A stranger approaches.
"Do you want a transfer? free."
Your eyes meet his and there is
the recognition,
like a laugh, like a kiss,
two Jews.
A sheynem dank for your *mitzvah*," you say.
"*Zei gezunt*," he says*
as the bus comes along. You get on.
A free transfer
to *Yiddishkayt*.

And you. walk about the city streets:
Seventh Avenue flowing with American Jews
like a river seeking an ocean;
in Chinatown, the gravestones of the old
  Sephardic cemetery
stare at neon lights on Friday nights;
in Williamsburg, bearded chassidim are busy
obeying 613 commandments;
on Fifth Avenue, the Rothschilds of America
daven in faultless English.

---

* "Thank you," "Be well"

Isidore Century

And you walk about the city streets
the stones of Masada hot beneath your feet.

What is it? What is it?
You have made your visit
and returned with questions
dancing on your head as on the ancient pin;
what is it the Jews?
a tribe? a nation? a race? a religion?
What is it the Torah, Mishnah, Gemarah?
What is it Masada, Kishinev, Treblinka?
And what does it matter to you,
an American Jew without portfolio?
It matters.

Even without *kashruth*,
it matters.
Even without God,
it matters.
Even without *shabbes*, synagogue,
it matters.
(May God bless you Izzy Vinegar everywhere,
he, the only Jew, and an Indian guide no less,
in a small Maine town on the Canadian border),
it matters.
It matters *Yom Kippur*,
it matters you do not convert,
it matters you are circumcised,
it matters Israel,
it matters, it matters, it matters.

Poems of Wonder and Wandering

A Lubavitcher beside a *mitzvah* truck asks,
"Are you a Jew? *Du bist a Yid?*"
and what is the glue?
your grandfather was a *misnagid*?
and where do you begin?
It is too late for *cheder*.
Poland is in ashes. In Israel
the questions dancing on your head
were irrelevant,
a Jewish joke about an elephant.
The answer without the question
is sufficient. You
are different enough
to be thrown in an oven.
And you walk about the city streets
the stones of Masada hot, hot, hot
beneath your feet.

One day, on Essex Street,
a rabbi is browsing beside you.
He introduces himself,
Rabbi Nachman of Breslov.
You have read his stories, maybe?
"*Sorry, no.*"
"Better. How can I help you?"
You do not know what you are looking for.
He has something.
what is it?
Don't ask.
He places a paper in your hand and leaves.
At the Garden Cafeteria, you look:

Isidore Century

a biblical map of Judea.
And it is clear,
you were only waiting for a sign to appear,
and soon you are flying above the clouds
with a map you cannot read
with a dream you have not yet dreamed,
eating a piece of honey cake
shared with you by a fellow passenger,
a rabbi,
with a black patch over one eye.

Nigun

A visitor to Chassidim,
I sang
yi di di di di,
yi di di di di de.
The song transported me
to a place
I had never been,
and yet I knew it.

I had traveled very far.
I had traveled very near,
and returned to a place of returning,

When later I learned the words,
they did not carry me
where now I longed to be.
It was a *yi* and a *di* and a *de,*
that note by note
and rung by rung
transported me
to a place
of infinite mercy.

Isidore Century

Simchas Torah

You heard of Simchas Torah
but never visited.
When you arrived
you were surprised;
dancing in the streets!
Torahs,
crowned with silver and gold,
robed in velvet, blue and scarlet,
bobbing up and down
like buoys in a sea of yarmulkes.
Such a hullabaloo
over a book of do's and don't's.
You were like a poor relation
invited to a wedding
who had borrowed a navy blue suit
too long in the sleeves.
And yet, you fit into the circle of dancers
whirling and whirling around a Torah
in a centrifuge
separating the holy and not yet holy,
and for one transcendental moment
you became an observant Jew
for the rest of your life.

The Shema

I said the *Shema*.
The *Shema* did not hear me; he
was standing across the road
from the Jaffa Gate waiting
for the light
to change from day to night
And when darkness fell,
as silently as a gang of kidnappers
upon the Old City walls,
he disappeared
in a black cloud of Chassidim
rushing to say their evening prayers.

I wandered through the Jewish quarter
like a herring out of water
asking if anyone had seen the *Shema*.
Yeshiva *buchers* laughed,
wigged women ran,
an elderly Chassid screamed GEVALT!

I fled from the confines of *mitzvot*
to the Wall,
the Wall accepts us all,
and there I prayed to a God
in whom I did not believe
to show me the way
to the *Shema*; he
appeared at my side
and called me by my Hebrew name,
Yitzhak.
We began the learning.

Isidore Century

A Guest, in Time

No strangers they
I sit and pray
with the Black Coats.
Kaddish is Kaddish,
a *minyan* is a *minyan*,
when a tenth man is needed
a cafeteria Jew will do.
Not, however, as a guest
at a *Shabbes* table.
As a *shiddach*
I am an untouchable.

I say my prayers,
they say theirs.
We are like two tribes
living under one roof,
eating from the same pot,
who once met in time,
and will meet again
beyond time
at a table where He
will take strict accountings.

Poems of Wonder and Wandering

Fresh Vegetables

Like fresh vegetables
I carry my sins
home from the market each day,
and cook up a sinner's stew
from a remorseful recipe
of my own making.
As I stand over the bubbling pot
I recall the saying of a Hasidic rabbi:
`Every sin contains within it
the seed of a good deed.'
In the aloneness of my atonement,
I suffer the joys
of my repentant meals.

Isidore Century

On Finding an Old Siddur

What becomes of prayers?
Three times a day, my grandmother, my
  grandfather.
Thousands of years,
Thousands of grandmothers, grandfathers.
Jerusalem, Spain, Poland,
everywhere
the same prayers.
Did they disappear
into nothingness?
Or remain in the air,
like holy nutrients
waiting for grandchildren
to gather them in,
and by praying them,
answer the prayers of our grandmothers, our
  grandfathers.

Poems of Wonder and Wandering

Messages

I wanted to make a sacrifice
like in the olden days,
but it is forbidden to bring Him
a bullock or sheep or goat.
So I asked Him if He wanted,
I would bring Him
a bagel with lox and cream cheese.
He didn't want.
"Better you should have it," He said.
Who am I to argue with God?

I say the blessing over the washing of the hands.
I say the blessing over the bagel.
And as I chew over my half-kosher pickle of resolve
to become observant, I hear two messages:
it's hard to be a Jew;
and something new,
it's lucky to be a Jew.

Isidore Century

Parallel Lines Never Meet

As I lingered at lakeside, the sun,
like a doctor on house call,
climbed up the back of the mountain on the opposite
  shore
to heal the sky of shadows;
the mist, like a sleeping giant
clad in a steamy grey sweat suit, awoke
and slowly rose from its water bed
to disappear into dawn.
A fisherman in a red canoe cast out his line,
a loon nearby dove down into deep waters.
'An Adirondack Garden of Eden,' I thought.
But the headlines lying on my lap,
a suicide/homicide bomber,
twenty Jews killed in Jerusalem,
transported me to a terminal of trains to nowhere,
there, to be rescued by the Bratzlaver Rabbi Nachman;
"*Gevalt*," he shouted. "Do not despair.
It is a *mitzvah* to be joyous always."
And as the fisherman reeled in a catch,
as the loon resurfaced with a fish in its beak,
I recalled a dream I had
of Sigmund Freud laying *tefillin* and saying,
"Hope and despair travel beside each other,
like parallel lines racing against death.
We must remember,
there is an exception to every rule.
Parallel lines will meet
in the world to come,
at a terminal in infinity."

Poems of Wonder and Wandering

Birds

Barefoot, I
am laying *tefillin*
on the beach at Coney Island.
No constant visitor here,
or to prayer,
I have taken flight
from the stuffy, recirculating prayers
in the basement synagogue
on Kingston Avenue.

Ancestors of old, exiled,
arriving, like storm-tossed terns
on some foreign shore,
similarly prayed.

A black-winged sea gull
pacing back and forth before me
must be wondering
what a strange bird I am;
black leather markings on arm and head,
striped black and white coat
over back and shoulders.
If I had wings
I would become a Jewish bird and fly
closer to God
and lay *tefillin* in the sky.

Isidore Century

Shabbes, Central Park

No *Shabbes* observer I
am observed by *Shabbes*
ride
to synagogue on a bus,
and after morning service
buy
a bagel and coffee at a corner stand.
No Kiddush for me.
Though drawn to traditional ways,
being confined by prayer for hours,
stained glass windows and dome notwithstanding,
is overmuch for this half-baked matzoh of a Jew.

Sitting on a bench, beneath an ordinary sky,
it is *Shabbes* also. I share it
and the bagel with sparrows who have no day of rest;
every day it is life and death
for a piece of bread.
And though *Shabbes* may not agree
I am doing a *mitzvah*, God,
who created *Shabbes*,
created sparrows too,
and a non-observant Jew to feed them.

Poems of Wonder and Wandering

Egrets

As the train raced across the Jersey swampland
I counted two, then three.
They reminded me of my Uncle Dave and Aunt Sadie:
They stood in the water
like white garden ornaments.
I rarely see them fly.
Perhaps they share a collective memory
of when they were slaughtered in their nesting areas
for their then-fashionable feathers,
and they have learned the old Yiddish saying,
makht nisht kayn geruder,
don't attract attention.
I remember my Uncle Dave telling me
the first time he had seen Aunt Sadie:
at a party on Rivington Street,
she made her entrance in a wide-brimmed red hat
with a long egret feather that seemed to flutter
in his direction.
He did not remember much else,
but his impulsive vow to marry her,
which he did.

Isidore Century

Believing Is Also A Mystery

Far from belief,
I hope in God,
who may be as near and far
as my prayers can reach.

In the old joke, a man
keeps running after a woman
until she catches him:
I keep running from a God
in whom I do not believe,
hoping he catches me.

Passover at the
Brooklyn Botanical Gardens

They do not serve matzah at the Terrace Cafe;
I have brought *shmurah* matzah,
a gift from the Lubavitchers
for past and future donations.
By some trick of tradition,
I am grateful I can afford to contribute,
yet feel guilty for not giving more.

I buy a side dish of tuna salad
to make a *matzah* sandwich.
It tastes of holiness and sin,
not unlike sweet and sour kosher Chinese shrimp.
I wonder if I'll get credit in the World to Come
for a half-*mitzvah*.
Can you be half-kosher for Passover?
Can you be half-Jewish?

Beyond the tulip beds a Black-crowned Night
  Heron
perches at the edge of the lily pond.
His crown is like a *yarmulke*,
his head , bent down close to the water,
shuckles, as though he is praying
to God for help to catch a goldfish swimming by.
I throw a few pieces of matzah towards him,
Manna from heaven!
He eats the *matzah*.
I eat my sandwich.
We're having a seder.

Isidore Century

Silent Tashlich

When all your purposes crumble,
and high intentions lie
like broken dishes at your feet,
take to oceans for repair.
If an ocean is not handy,
a pond or stream will do.
Once there,
say nothing to birds,
they have their own concerns;
cry not to little fishes,
their bones are too brittle
to withstand despair;
do not confide in clouds,
they are as fickle as fashion.
All that is required
is your attention to water.

Glossary

amidah – the silent, central prayer in the service

bar mitzvah – Jewish boy's coming-of-age at 13

bobbe – grandmother

brucha – blessing

cholent – savory dish of meat, potatoes and beans put up before the Sabbath so that one can have hot food for lunch without violating the prohibition against Sabbath cooking

chachem – wise man. When said sarcastically, it means the reverse!

cheder – Hebrew School, lit., "room"

chutzpah – arrogance, nerve

davening – praying

Eshet Hayil – "Woman of Valor"; the Biblical passage of Proverbs 31

farbissener – bitter or sour-faced

gevaldik – wonderful

gemutlich – warm and congenial; pleasant and friendly, amiable, kindly

gemutlichkeit –the quality of being *gemutlich*

HaShem – lit., "The Name," a respectful way to refer to God

Hasid – a Jew that worships in an emotional ecstatic manner in order to get close to God (plural: *Hasidim*, adjective: *Hasidic*)

Kaddish – prayer recited by mourners

kiddush – blessing over wine that sanctifies the Sabbath and other holidays

kashruth – kosherness

kugel – Eastern European casserole
kvitles – notes to God left in the Western Wall
matzah – unleavened bread eaten on Passover
matzah brei – Passover dish of eggs and *matzah*
mazel – luck
megillah – scroll, Book of Esther, convoluted story
meshuggeners – crazy people
midrash – rabbinic elaboration on a Biblical story
mincha – afternoon prayers
minhag – custom
minyan – prayer quorum of ten
mishpocheh – family
misnagid – not a *hasid*
momzer – bastard
nigun – a (usually wordless) melody
nu? – so?
rebbe – Rabbi
schnapps – hard liquor
Shabbes – the Sabbath; Saturday
Shekhinah – the Divine Presence
Shema – prayer attesting to God's oneness
shidduch – match, arranged marriage
shlepper – carrier, one who is burdened, a *shnook*
shnorrers – beggars
souk – marketplace
shtetl – Eastern European hamlet
shtibl – small synagogue, often located in
   someone's house
shuckled – swayed back and forth in prayer
shul – synagogue
tallis (talleisim) – prayer shawl(s)

Glossary

tefillin – leather amulets worn during prayer

teshuvah – repentance; returning to God and
  Judaism

tsaddik – a righteous man; a saint

tzedaka – charity; alms

yarmulke – skull cap

yeshiva – Jewish religious academy

yeshiva bucher – a yeshiva student; a young
  rabbinical scholar

yichus – family ties; connections to a good family
  that make for a desirable match

Yid (Yidden) – Jew (Jews)

yiddish – to speak "Jewish" a composite language
  of German and Hebrew

Yiddishkayt – Jewishness

zei gezunt – Be healthy! Often used as a farewell
  greeting

Glossary

from the Coffee House
of Jewish Dreamers

*Poems of
Wonder and Wandering*

Isidore Century

Ben Yehuda Press
Teaneck, NJ